D0730598

Stranger to the Truth

LISA C. HICKMAN

AuthorHouse™
1663 Liberty Drive
Bloomington, IN 47403
www.authorhouse.com
Phone: 1-800-839-8640

Cover photograph by Dave Darnell.

On October 6, 2005, Noura Jackson was in court where she pleaded not guilty to first-degree murder in the stabbing death of her mother, Jennifer Jackson.

Published by AuthorHouse 10/18/2013

ISBN: 978-1-4918-1339-3 (sc)
ISBN: 978-1-4918-1337-9 (hc)
ISBN: 978-1-4918-1338-6 (e)

Library of Congress Control Number: 2013915445

This book is printed on acid-free paper.

For Jess

It seems to me that every thing in the light and air ought to be happy.

Whoever is not in his coffin and the dark grave let him know he has enough.

—Walt Whitman, "The Sleepers"

You think that life is nothing but not being stone dead. . . . But to shut me from the light of the sky and the sight of the fields and flowers; . . . and keep me from everything that brings me back to the love of God . . . : all this is worse than the furnace in the Bible that was heated seven times. . . . if only I could hear the wind in the trees, the larks in the sunshine . . . and the blessed blessed church bells . . . But without these things I cannot live; and by your wanting to take them away from me, or from any human creature, I know that your counsel is of the devil, and that mine is of God.

—Bernard Shaw, *Saint Joan*

TABLE OF CONTENTS

PREFACE

Noura's story came to me through my daughter. Her path briefly had crossed Noura's during high school at St. Agnes Academy. That Sunday morning, June 5, 2005, in the aftermath of the Memphis Italian Festival, she told me Noura's mother, Jennifer, had been killed. Jennifer and Noura's home was not far from the site of Italian Fest or from our East Memphis residence. After the murder, it seemed like I couldn't go anywhere without driving by their New Haven address.

Rumors flew almost immediately that Noura, eighteen years old, was responsible. My elder son's friend, a bond trader, worked closely with Jennifer at SunTrust Bank. Jennifer had talked to him about her problems with Noura and told him she was drug testing her. One day after the murder, he came to our house with a friend of his, Jennifer's brother, Eric.

Eric obviously was reeling from grief. At one point on June 5, when Noura returned to the house she had shared with her mom, she said, "Who will clean up this mess?" Eric shook his head in disbelief as he related that story. The more I heard, the more incredulous I became. Matricide—if that's what had happened—wasn't a common occurrence. The word itself was startling.

Several years before, I had reviewed a Judith Rossner novel, *Perfidia* (Spanish for betrayal). Rossner fictionalized the real-life story of a young girl whose acceptance to Harvard was rescinded when the college discovered she had committed matricide. In her novel, Rossner depicted the mother as emotionally, verbally, and physically abusive to her daughter. I wasn't hearing anything similar about Jennifer and Noura.

A book was an incipient idea but gathering momentum. It was what I couldn't reconcile that propelled the writing project. A group of teenagers, partying, and yes, being reckless and difficult. And one member, a young girl, accused of murdering her mother, because in theory, her mom started saying no to this life style. The twinning of this normal and extremely abnormal behavior suggested a compelling and worthwhile book. I had no way of knowing just how compelling or that my involvement with the story would span eight years.

After Noura's arrest in September 2005, I began going downtown when she had a court appearance. I realized I was fairly committed when I regularly made it to court on the days when Noura's name was on the docket. It's an arduous process, getting into 201 Poplar when the doors open. A line circles the building. At that time I was teaching writing and literature at Christian Brothers University. I had some homicide detectives in my classes. One officer in particular would meet me or send a friend to help me bypass the long line. Noura's court dates for motions, hearings, and other legal maneuverings went on for three and a half years.

I never fully understood why Noura's trial was so delayed. Over the course of three-plus years, besides attending her court dates, I was reading and researching. I also was getting to know some of Noura's supporters, observing Jennifer's family and advocates, and becoming acquainted with how the defense and prosecution squared off. Finally a trial date was set for February 2009. When the trial started it unleashed a watershed of information. The story I already considered important and fascinating was revealed to be that and so much more.

During one of the early pretrial dates, a courtroom bailiff stationed at the door asked everyone who entered whose case they were attending. Noura turned when I said her name, and not recognizing me, she gave me a cool and puzzled look. As time went on, she apparently grew accustomed to my presence. When the day finally arrived to select a jury, a Memphis television correspondent focused her coverage on Noura's solitude. "It was clear . . . she had no family anywhere nearby," Kontji Anthony reported. "The only people in or outside the courtroom were court staffers, potential jurors, a national TV show, and a book author." Who would have imagined Noura's trial would be one of Shelby County's most complex and expensive?

The Memphis newspaper, *The Commercial Appeal*, offered some excellent coverage of Noura's situation. As I began reading, researching, and developing sources, I started to explore ways to frame Jennifer and Noura's story. I decided the book would be narrative nonfiction. And when I actually started writing, it became clear fairly quickly that the narrative would not easily be tamed. It did not conform to a linear telling or a consistent point of view. Noura's point of view is represented as well as Jennifer's point of view.

There also is the outside point of view—the thoughts and opinions about Noura and Jennifer derived from others. I gathered much of this material from interviews and trial testimony. What might be considered the "outside outside" point of view is the anonymous online bloggers. Noura's case generated intense interest and intense emotions. I chronicled some of these feelings by using online blog posts. They added another dimension, color, and sometimes even humor to the story.

When Jennifer and Noura's home was on the market, I was able to look around the house. Like many homes in Memphis, it is a classic, one-level ranch built in the mid-1950s. You enter the front of the house by way of a small foyer. To the left from the foyer is one long hall that leads to three bedrooms and a common bathroom; to the right are the kitchen and other living areas. It seemed the sunroom that looked out on the backyard and pool probably was an addition. My walk-through was tangible and therefore helpful as I thought about the family who had lived there and the events that later transpired.

The house was empty except for some stacked boxes that seemed to represent Noura's childhood library or at least part of it. The boxes all were marked with the same year, 1997, and neatly labeled: Books—Noura's Youth, Walt Disney Books, Fairy Tales and Game Books. Other boxes contained what might be considered a young girl's treasures: stuffed animals, some Beanie Babies, and keepsakes. I also noticed Jennifer's books on parenting and rearing a gifted child.

I remember the shock of the backyard. It was as if people had been sitting around the pool and suddenly got up and walked off. The pool had a green cover haphazardly thrown over it, the center of which had given way and was weighed down by stale water and leaves. There was an eerie and ill-kempt covered walkway in the backyard that accessed a confusing array of doors.

After the trial concluded, Judge Craft, who was extremely helpful throughout, allowed me to review the photographs placed in evidence. Photographer Lance Murphy met me in Judge Craft's office, and he and I selected a number of images that he photographed. Having those to use as a reference source proved valuable. It was necessary but painful to look at the photographs of Jennifer to describe the position of her body on the bedroom floor.

When you're involved with a subject for a number of years, it permeates your subconscious. About midway through this book I had a vivid dream about Jennifer that was impossible to shake or forget. She stood beside my bedside (later I couldn't help but think how I also sleep on the left side) and seemed to have something to say. In the end, all I remember is her breath which was an icy blast. The disturbing dream made me keenly aware of her suffering. And *that* probably was her message.

This book has never had a tendentious intent. My goal always was to stay objective and follow the story as it unraveled; and like most good stories, there were many threads to follow. I conducted the interviews dispersed throughout the book unless otherwise indicated. Other sources range from pretrial appearances, motions, and hearings; jury selection; the fourteen-day trial and trial testimony; the sentencing trial; the motion for a new trial; research on matricide; broadcast, print, and online media; and the ruling of the Tennessee Court of Criminal Appeals.

Regardless of the tone or point of view, the story is built around research and facts. What, for example, Noura might be thinking is not idle conjecture but based on material I gathered from research. Perhaps it was a detail someone recounted in an interview or information from courtroom testimony.

I wanted to end the book by offering readers my version of what happened that Saturday night (actually early Sunday morning). I was not inclined to believe in Noura's guilt or innocence. It took years of research, thought, and analysis to arrive at this depiction of events. The Epilogue is a synthesis of what I learned and came to believe possible. But as Noura's friend Andrew Hammack said in our interview, "The only people who will ever know are Noura and her mother."

PROLOGUE

The house itself was unremarkable but for its location which was betwixt and between. One side yard abutted a busy Memphis road dominated by the noise of passing cars, irritated drivers sounding their horns, and deafening sirens from the nearby fire station, while the other side yard merged easily into the quiet East Memphis neighborhood. The situation of the occupants, a mother and daughter, wasn't very different. Volatile quarrels or silent truces characterized Jennifer and Noura's home life.

Jennifer realized giving up on her relationship with Noura would be the hardest thing she ever did in her life. She loved her daughter so much. Her world practically had revolved around Noura. And when she remembered her as a little girl, how affectionate and sweet she had been, Jennifer felt her heart crumple. Those books she'd read on rearing a gifted child seemed useless now. It felt as if she'd done everything wrong as a mom. Noura's rebellion was out of control. She was making Jennifer's life miserable. Sullen, pouting, resentful, and always mad.

Sometimes the way Noura looked at her made Jennifer realize she'd already lost her. It was as if Noura didn't care if she ever saw her again. That hurt more than the yelling and storming off she would do. Jennifer knew the teenage years were tough, but she finally admitted to herself she couldn't live with Noura anymore. Noura had defied her again tonight; she had gone out partying when she was grounded. Tomorrow Jennifer would tell her she had to leave. Boarding school, military, she didn't care what, Noura couldn't stay in this house. Searing pain gripped her at the thought of turning her daughter out, and she wondered if she would have the courage.

When she got home later there would be another fight. It was Saturday night and she was supposed to spend it catching up on schoolwork?! Crazy! Noura was sick of her mom's interference. She'd decided Noura's friends were bad influences and that she "needed a new group." Everyone and everything she cared about her mom disliked. Jennifer had run off the only guy she'd ever loved. He'd be at the party tonight and she hoped they'd make up.

Noura couldn't believe the way her mom had turned her life upside down! She gave her a curfew and went ballistic when she was late. Nagged and nagged about Noura's schoolwork. She'd scream if her mom asked her one more time about drugs! Why did she suddenly care if she smoked weed? It wasn't a secret. She had actually drug tested her! Her own daughter! They wrangled over every little thing she wanted to buy. She had no money to call her own. Sometimes Noura didn't know herself. The hard, ugly thoughts she felt and the anger broiling in her head.

Part I

Author's Note

The online blog comments included in this book are represented as they appeared in their original medium. The spelling often is incorrect, and frequently the grammar is nonstandard. This also is true of the various witness statements and other primary sources collected here.

The Memphis Italian Festival's sixteenth year in 2005 would be widely remembered for its connection to Jennifer Jackson's homicide.

Italian Fest

Q: When is the last time you spoke with your mom?
A: At 12:10 this morning.

Q: Did you go to the Italian Fest last evening on Saturday night?
A: Yes.

Q: Is that in Marquette Park?
A: Yes.

Q: Who is Perry?
A: He's like my boyfriend, but we've been on and off lately . . . we've been on and off for about a year.

Q: What did you do after you spoke with your mom?
A: Hung out at Perry's a little longer . . . 30 minutes, then they took me back to my car and I went and got cigarettes, then I went to Taco Bell, then I realized I didn't have my wallet, I called Perry to asked him to look around his house for it, so I went back to Carter's and found my wallet, then I bought gas, I have a receipt for that. Then I drove to Cordova to Eric Whittakers (sic), but decided to head on home, we talked for a minute

though. I was talking to Andrew Hammack on the phone. He was going to stop by my house and see my kitten and we were supposed to talk. I was supposed to call him when I got home, but I found what I found.—
Noura Jackson's Witness Statement, June 5, 2005

It was the last sliver of the summer afternoon. That lazy, tired time of day between the promise of morning and the possibility of evening. Two teenagers—listening distractedly to a local radio station—made their way across town. Noura Jackson, the driver, was calculating how to outmaneuver her mother. Her mom would tell her *again* that she was grounded until she finished her schoolwork. That would mean staying home tonight—a Saturday. Not likely to happen as far as Noura was concerned. Her passenger, Kaole (pronounced Cole) Madison, who was still a little stoned, glanced at Noura, puzzled by her subdued mood. After all, they looking forward to a preparty, kicking off what should be an even better party.

"Damn," Noura said. "My mom's still there. I don't want to go home now. I don't feel like dealing with her."

Noura also had a nice buzz from the mellow time they'd had that afternoon. The last thing she wanted now was to see her mom, which would lead to conflict—another argument about her lack of responsibility—she just knew it. Sometimes it seemed they had been fighting forever though she knew that wasn't really true. But something had shifted. Suddenly finishing her GED work and curfews were a big deal. And all her friends, especially her boyfriend,

Perry, were suspect. She was threatening—promising—to get a restraining order against him!

She loved her mom, but right now she wanted to be as far away from her as possible. Jennifer was treating Noura more like a child than ever, even drug testing her. She was eighteen years old, and since her father's death over a year ago, she should have been completely independent. She was his only heir, yet her mom controlled the money. How many arguments had they had about that? Too many, even Noura knew. If her mom would give her what was hers, she'd move out and perhaps one day they would be all right again.

"Why don't we check out parking for Italian Fest tonight?" Noura suggested. "Maybe by the time we get back she'll be gone." Kaole didn't ask Noura any questions about why she didn't want to see her mom. Such situations were all too common among himself and his friends and their parents. Seemed like there were so many things to argue about: curfews, rules, cars, money, drinking, work, school, and friends. The list just went on and on.

Noura knew her mom was going to the wedding of a friend's daughter that night with Jimmy Tual, whom Noura regarded as a socialite. Jimmy escorted Jennifer when she and Mark Irvin, her Methodist minister boyfriend, were off again. God what a prick Mark is, Noura thought again. And a creep! Always trying to look down her shirt. It would be good if this time the breakup really lasted.

They'd already made one stop since leaving Kaole's house. At a friend's house Noura borrowed a hair dryer. It was midafternoon as they circled through her East Memphis neighborhood in Noura's Jeep Cherokee. They passed a sign in front of one nearby house advertising free kittens. That would be sweet, Noura thought, a little kitten to play with, something new. Her mom probably wouldn't think so but so what. Soon she hoped to be living on her own anyway.

They headed toward Eastgate Shopping Center, a strip mall near Noura's house, where they picked up beer at an Ike's Pharmacy and scouted parking for later that night. The shopping center, across the street from Marquette Park, offered ideal parking for the popular, three-day Memphis Italian Festival that drew throngs of local teens.

Part festival, part carnival, part arts and crafts fair, part rock and roll venue, Italian Fest is an amalgamation probably only Memphians could understand. Dotted throughout the park are individual tents outfitted as Italian kitchens (there were forty-seven teams in 2011). Varying in degrees of flamboyance and creativity, the cooking teams' tents host private parties serving Italian food and also beer and liquor. An easy venue for underage drinkers. The 2005 festivities fell on June 2, 3, and 4, Thursday through Saturday nights, and drew from all age groups. Many of the attendees were Catholic school students from St. Agnes Academy, Immaculate Conception, Christian Brothers High School, and St. Benedict. Holy Rosary's parish school benefits from the event's proceeds, but odds were teenagers passing through the gates were more focused on partying than altruism.

The festival's sixteenth year would be widely remembered for the shocking awakening on Sunday morning when word spread far and wide across Memphis of a horrific homicide. Jennifer Jackson, a beautiful, thirty-nine-year-old bond trader, was discovered dead by a neighbor and Jennifer's eighteen-year-old daughter, Noura. Jennifer had been stabbed more than fifty times in her East Memphis home about a mile and a half from Marquette Park.

Like her daughter's, the night of June 4 had been a social one for Jennifer. In spite of a rough start—a disheartening phone conversation that morning with her boyfriend, Mark—the evening involved good company. Her close friend Jimmy stepped into the lurch left by Mark, and together they attended Molly Fuller's wedding. Molly was the daughter of Jennifer's friend, Mary Jane Fuller. At 5:30 p.m. Jennifer arrived at Tual's East Memphis home on Charleswood, about a mile from her own New Haven address. Tual drove to the 6 p.m. wedding ceremony at Calvary Episcopal Church in Downtown Memphis. Then it was back to East Memphis for the wedding reception held at the bride's parents' home on Williamsburg Lane. Jennifer and Jimmy, along with fifty or so other guests, mingled and enjoyed the evening. They stayed about two hours, and though alcohol was served, Jimmy said Jennifer was not intoxicated.

Before calling it a night, Jimmy and Jennifer stopped at a neighborhood bar, the Cockeyed Camel, for a drink. Jennifer called her friend Linda Finlay, who lived in Cordova, an outlying area of Memphis, to meet them. "I talked with her that night and she wanted me to meet her at the Cockeyed Camel," Finlay said. "I didn't go because I'd had too much to drink to drive. If I had gone, I would have spent the night at Jennifer's house. I wouldn't have driven back to Cordova."

Jennifer paid their bar tab with her credit card—11:06 p.m. was the last time the card was swiped—and Tual then drove back to Charleswood. They said goodnight outside, and Jennifer got in her car and left around 11:30 p.m. Tual said there was nothing unusual about Jennifer's behavior that night. He never saw her alive again.

"People were just inordinately sad about Jennifer's death. She was just extremely well liked," he said. "She was such a fair person. A caring, generous friend who was always positive and upbeat."

Party Circuit

Defense attorney Art Quinn told the jury in his opening statement that they would meet a lot of "East Memphis brats."

Presiding Criminal Court Judge Christopher Craft observed the young people as "very privileged, completely selfish and out of control."

"They called me to do 48 Hours *and I said, 'No way.' I knew they would make me look like a party girl or a complete bratty private school kid that used all my parents' money to party and act inappropriately. What about the good things that all of us do?"—Sophie Cooley to journalist Lauren Lee*

The Saturday of the Italian Festival weekend unfolded in a leisurely fashion. Noura didn't work outside of a little babysitting here and there, and was not doing much in the way of school that summer. Late on Saturday morning, she picked up a friend, Alex Kline, at Alex's dad's former house. It was empty and a good place to party. They might smoke some weed there in case Kaole's parents were around when they got to his place. Noura, like many her age, smoked a good bit of marijuana, at least three days a week just with Kaole. "It was a pretty regular thing for all of us kids," said her friend, Sophie Cooley. She recalls smoking with Noura and others by Noura's swimming pool, though never in front of Jennifer Jackson. This afternoon, though, they planned to spend the day by Kaole's pool. These times were all about partying, going out, getting high, and drama. Drama queens was Kaole's name for Noura's girlfriends—"They liked to stir up trouble." Though the same could be said of almost all high-school girls. They inhabited a scene typified by competition, status, jealousies, and insecurities.

On the way to Kaole's house, Noura and Alex were scheming about hooking him up with a girl they knew had caught his attention. Maybe inviting her to Kaole's to swim as well. They made another brief stop at Noura's house where she ran in to get her swimsuit. She was quick, planning to avoid her mom altogether. At least I can find something in my room, Noura thought. That house, it's a wreck, bedlam.

The exterior brick of Jennifer and Noura's three-bedroom ranch at 5001 New Haven was painted unimaginative beige. It resembled many East Memphis homes built in the mid-1950s; a one-level ranch with hardwood floors throughout. The kitchen and bathrooms had not been noticeably updated. A solid home in a nice area though one side of the house ran parallel to a busy street. But unlike many similar homes, Jennifer and Noura's home was swamped by clutter.

"My sister," Grace France said of Jennifer, "was not the best housekeeper." Magazines, newspapers, books, shoes, clothes, purses, and assorted random items covered almost every surface. The shower rod in Jennifer's bathroom off her bedroom served as another clothing rack (it didn't appear to have been used as a shower for some time) and the bathroom floor was reinvented as a second closet for shoes. The bedroom floor was littered with clothes, shoes, handbags, and odds and ends.

Another entire bedroom, painted bright maroon with some lighter pink shades, had been converted to a closet. It was something you might see in a second-hand store with clothes hanging from rows of metal clothing rods. A successful bond trader with SunTrust Capital Markets, Jennifer's shopping was legendary. "She piled up on everything" her brother, Eric Sherwood, said. "She was a pack rat. Sometimes she would be in the middle of cleaning up, and other times it would be a mess." Jennifer made multiple purchases of the same item from Williams-Sonoma or warehouse places like Costco. Boxes would never be opened. Overflow from the house spilled into the garage that was shelved from top to bottom. When that was full, Jennifer rented multiple storage units. The one exception to all the clutter, at least on occasion, was Noura's khaki bedroom. A refuge of sort from the surrounding chaos.

The girls showed up at Kaole's house about 11:00 a.m. recouping from the night before. One of their friends, Carter

Kobeck, lived within walking distance of the festival site. The usual group of friends had met at his house for a prefestival party Friday night and planned to again Saturday. It was convenient to have a central location so close to Marquette Park. Kaole didn't recall anything too out of the ordinary about Friday night at Carter's place except Noura coming in the kitchen and asking for a band aid. Whether for herself or someone else he didn't know. After a few hours at Carter's, the group dispersed. "By then," Kaole said, "we had a pretty nice buzz so we walked to the Italian Fest."

While Kaole did yard work—taking periodical breaks to hang out with the girls—Alex and Noura got some sun by the pool. They recently had rekindled their friendship after meeting in the eighth grade at Ridgeway, a Memphis public school. (Prior to Ridgeway, Noura had been at St. Agnes Academy, St. Mary's Episcopal School—both all-girls' schools—and Lausanne Collegiate School in Memphis, as well as attending schools in Arkansas and Atlanta, Georgia.) Noura left Ridgeway her junior year to attend St. George's Independent School though by the end of the school year she was enrolled in a home-school program. Noura planned to return to Ridgeway for her senior year or perhaps get a GED.

Kaole also struggled with traditional schools, and after a few tries at various high schools, finished his high-school course work through Gateway, a Christian-based, home-school program. Kaole encouraged Noura to stick with Gateway, which he liked and found lenient. His aunt was his teacher. Plus, it was accredited and students finished with a real diploma. Noura was more interested in getting a GED. Easier, she thought. School—Gateway, Ridgeway, or any other—was just another point of contention. Since she'd lost interest in Gateway, her participation waned. She and her mom had been round and round about that!

Kaole and Noura's friendship had been consistent since they met their freshman year of high school. They had a bit of a crush on each other, but Noura wound up dating his best friend, Perry Brasfield. Kaole has a full head of curly blond hair and an open, engaging manner. They'd been friends now for years, seeing each other nearly every day, smoking weed and partying. They smoked often at Noura's house, "More times than I could count on two hands," Kaole said. Once, a few years earlier, Noura's mom came home unexpectedly and caught them smoking in the backyard. Even after that, Jennifer never made him feel unwelcome in her home. She even made a few jokes about it later on. Kaole knew Jennifer tried to set curfews that Noura rarely followed. He didn't remember Noura caring much if her mom was upset about it either.

Kaole, Noura, and their group's drug use intensified after their friend Anna Menkel was killed in a car accident in January 2005. Anna had been a junior at St. Agnes Academy where she and Noura met in the seventh grade. With her best friend's sudden death, Noura spiraled into a deep depression. She memorialized her friend with a delicate colored tattoo in cursive on the top of her foot that simply said *Anna*.

Jennifer seemed to understand how much Anna's death hurt her daughter, though she expressed her sympathy in a curiously phrased note. On Noura's Valentine's card the year of Anna's passing, Jennifer remarked on Anna's loss of *Noura*. More commonly, Noura would have been consoled on the tragic loss of her close friend. "Dear Noura," Jennifer wrote, "how unfortunate Anna was in her short life to have lost a friend like you. You have so much love to give."

Dana Fredrick, Ph.D., life-long educator, and mother of Noura's close friends, Lindsey and Natalie Fredrick, described Noura as "completely heartbroken by Anna's death." She was absolutely devastated and kept the eulogy [from Anna's service] in her pocket." But after Jennifer's death, Natalie observed to *Commercial Appeal* reporter Sherri Drake, "Noura was always like, 'I miss my mom,' but I could always tell there was something wrong because every time we talked about it, she'd just get real quiet."

Whether as a means of escape or teenage curiosity, the drugs got more serious, though never included methamphetamine or acid. The standard fare of marijuana and alcohol was enhanced with pharmaceuticals like Lortab, Xanax, and hydrocodone syrup, an opiate painkiller, used to treat a cough. Sophie recalled sipping the hydrocodone—which usually is mixed with alcohol and other ingredients—from a baby bottle, a practice the Memphis rap group Three 6 Mafia called "Sippin on Sizzurp." Xanax bars, white, bar-looking pills (usually two milligrams and scored three times), also were favored. Noura's friend Kirby McDonald said, "The bars give you a really good feeling with alcohol." Noura relied on Xanax bars for anxiety and stress, "It would help ease her emotions," Kaole said.

Less often they experimented with cocaine and psychedelic mushrooms, or "chocolates," as they were called when the mushrooms were ground and baked in a chocolate bar. Noura and Kaole took chocolates on two occasions, once in Noura's backyard with a group of people and once in Shady Grove Park. Kaole hadn't tried cocaine—didn't want to—and the time Noura did with friends in her living room, he watched TV and later fell asleep. "I didn't judge anybody about coke. I just wanted to set myself out," he said.

Noura also spent time with Andrew Hammack, an obvious outsider among the private school, East Memphis group. Few would mistake Andrew for Perry and his ilk, some of whom displayed a degree of polish. A lackluster high school student, Andrew later worked construction. His appearance and inexpensive haircut, along with his crass choice of words describing Noura and himself—"friends with benefits"—confirmed a different background. Andrew puzzled Noura's adult friends. They tried to discern how and why he was a part of her life and assumed he was her drug supplier.

Though Noura hadn't known him long compared with the others in her circle, she liked how different Andrew was from them. He understood her life in ways Perry couldn't. Andrew hadn't had everything handed to him. He wasn't "private school" or full of bullshit. His life was hardscrabble in many ways. Noura didn't feel Andrew looked down on her because of her dad's sketchy gas station and brushes with police. Being on the outside wasn't unusual for Andrew. He could accept difference in a way some of her friends couldn't.

Besides his legal wrangles, Nazmi Hassanieh, Noura's father, was Lebanese. That alone was too much for her mom's sisters, Noura thought. He was a foreigner, and they never had a decent word to say about him. Noura considered her aunts' rich, safe lives. There was no room for someone like Nazmi. They must have thought her mom was crazy when she married him.

Sometimes she caught a whiff of that from her friends as well. They sure didn't have a father from Lebanon who sold beer to underage teenagers. (She would have called her friends WASPs if most of them weren't Catholic. Ha.) As one mother remarked, "Noura was always the scapegoat. Mothers always blamed Noura, and their daughters encouraged it so *they* didn't get in trouble."

Sophie Cooley confirmed this, saying that "[Noura] was definitely always the girl that your parents didn't want you to hang out with. She was a little bit more mature than everybody else, developed before everybody else. She was the girl that your parents said, 'Maybe there's something a little off here.' But everyone still hung out with her anyway."

Just prior to Noura's seventeenth birthday in late January 2004, her forty-three-year-old father was murdered at his Memphis gas station and convenience store, Noura's Kwik Stop. Some people thought his involvement with a Mexican drug cartel was the real motive for his death, not a robbery at his gas station. The cartel was a deadly trafficking organization, and Nazmi had been shot the day before he was to testify in federal court. The homicide officers showed Noura and Jennifer the surveillance tape from the Kwik Shop. Nazmi clearly knew his killer; in fact, he came out from behind the counter to welcome him. The assassin took the videotape unaware of the backup tape.

Noura watched as her father greeted the killer, but the camera failed to capture the shooter's features. That was a year and a half ago, and the police had no suspects. Dana Fredrick told Jennifer during a phone conversation that Noura was "extremely traumatized by the death of her father." She knew Noura was grieving for her dad, especially when Noura brought a box of Nazmi's belongings to Dana's house and kept them there. Dana suggested Jennifer seek grief counseling for her daughter. There is no indication that Jennifer followed up on this suggestion or that Noura ever received any professional help.

Noura realized Nazmi probably was mixed up with drug dealers and prostitutes. She heard people speculate that his other business, Aladdin Limos, run from the same location as his gas station, ferried prostitutes and their clients to the casinos in Tunica, Mississippi, about forty miles south of Memphis. Conveniently enough, Noura's Kwik Stop was located directly in front of the strip club, Platinum Plus.

Strange how he came in and out of her life. ("In no meaningful way," her uncle Eric criticized. Well, that was his opinion, Noura thought.) Eight years passed without a glimpse of him, and then one night she used the restroom in his gas station and realized the short, friendly man at the register was her father! His store was well known for liberally selling beer to minors, in fact; that was exactly what brought Noura in there that night. She and her friends were only fifteen years old at the time.

Nazmi's relaxed attitude toward beer sales to young girls and relationships with underage females resulted in felony charges against him when he ran his restaurant in Mississippi—Nora's Catfish Place—prior to owning his gas station at 2534 Mount Moriah where he was killed. In 1993, he was charged with sexually molesting and serving alcohol to minor females in his employ at the restaurant. That same year he faced a felony assault charge involving a sixteen-year-old girl in Tennessee.

For Noura, much of the relationship with her father was bittersweet. Their reunion when she was fifteen was short-lived, and only a couple of years later he was gone forever. In many ways she knew she still was reeling from that abrupt parting.

And Anna. It hurt too much to think about her, though she could never stop herself. Noura waged war against her thoughts of Anna and her father all too frequently. When the feelings began to bubble up, she wanted to bury them; smoke some weed, take a Lortab, drink some beer, anything but directly face all that pain. She imagined that to her friends she seemed the quintessential party girl. That was her facade. Get good and wasted. She struggled to seem light spirited on the outside; inside she was anything but.

Andrew was good during her dark times. He helped her relax. When she and Perry would break up, Andrew was there. They even wound up in bed together. That was okay with Noura though nothing like being with Perry. Sometimes sex with Andrew only made her miss Perry more. Maybe Andrew was a little jealous of Perry, but he still stuck by her.

Noura was sure her mom—especially now that she was being ridiculous about who she hung out with—would object to Andrew. Jennifer had met him only once, though he said he sometimes saw her running in Audubon Park. He had been inside their house a few times when Jennifer was away. Usually he waited out front in his truck for Noura.

Andrew eventually mixed with Noura's circle of friends, though he said he never hung out with Perry. "Perry, Eric [Whitaker], and Joey [McGoff] were more her side of friends," he said. Andrew was friends with Kaole and Carter. He said he knew Sophie and knew Alex Kline quite well.

And he also observed Noura's sometimes fiery nature: "And she had a lot of friends. But one day they would be having fun and the next she would be calling them bitches," Andrew said in an interview. "Her friendships were rocky. Always a lot—*a lot*—of drama."

Andrew's association with Noura was not without its own drama. After Jennifer's death, homicide detectives asked him for a DNA sample and questioned him on three separate occasions. His accounts to police reveal conflicting details of his whereabouts and his time line for June 4 and

5. Andrew admitted in his handwritten third statement that he was “Rolling on XTC [ecstasy] that night,” and at a movie theatre mere blocks from the Jackson home.

“You didn’t want to make Noura mad,” Andrew said. “She had a temper. You could just be fooling around, being pranksters, and she might get mad, yell, have a hissy fit, and leave.”

Kirby McDonald said she and Noura fought a lot and and went long stretches without speaking. And before Italian Fest weekend of 2005, Kirby hadn’t seen Noura in a couple of weeks. In the past, though, Noura came through for her; she was the one Kirby called to take her to the hospital when she took an overdose of Tylenol.

Noura knew a little something about suicide attempts. In the seventh grade while celebrating a boy’s fourteenth birthday at an Embassy Suites Hotel, the kids were discovered smoking pot by the honoree’s father. The dad decided to let it go, but Noura described the event to a friend’s mother. The next thing Noura knew, she was ostracized, bad mouthed, and ignored by all the boys she had considered friends. In response, Noura also took an overdose of Tylenol. It was rumored to have been a suicide attempt. This strong reaction on Noura’s part to a teenage slight elucidates her later dependency on her friends. They mattered the most to her, even as early as the seventh grade.

Despite her sometimes angry outbursts, Andrew believed Noura needed friends more than most people—that she really counted on them—because she wasn't a family person, which was an opinion shared by Noura's aunt Grace. "Noura," Grace said, "was a distant teenager and didn't want to be part of the family events." But Grace acknowledged also that she wasn't close to her niece and that some years passed without her even seeing Noura.

Had they wanted on the afternoon of June 4, Noura, Alex, and Kaole could have gone swimming at Noura's house. A sunroom off the den looked out on a pool and backyard enclosed by a privacy fence. In happier times, the pool and yard were the site of celebrations—birthdays and holidays—and cookouts arranged by Jennifer. "Jennifer had people over to the house all the time," Eric said. "Friends and family." Noura's friends were often invited for meals and spent the night as well.

Kaole, who was very fond of Noura's mom, occasionally had dinner with Jennifer, and her boyfriend, Mark. Sometimes Kaole even did the grilling. But the latest gathering in the Jackson backyard caused such a fight it still rippled through Jennifer and Noura's relationship.

Family Reunion?

"Noura was sullen and wouldn't look anyone in the eye," her aunt Cindy said, describing the aftermath of an argument between Noura and Jennifer at her Florida home Memorial Day weekend 2005. "She was mad and upset." But later, Cindy thought, Noura looked sad.

"The void of Jennifer's absence cannot be filled. No holiday, birthday or family occasion will ever be quite the same. Jennifer was larger than life to us and to those who loved her. Not a day goes by that we are not all reminded in some way of the many and wonderful ways that Jennifer touched our lives and never will again."
—Victim Impact Statement

Memorial Day weekend of 2005, a week before Jennifer was murdered, was the second trip for Noura and her mom in just two months. For Noura's birthday in March Jennifer had surprised her with a trip to Florida. That brief period of harmony turned out to be the calm before the storm. No one was prepared for the maelstrom this trip to visit family would set in motion.

Usually Memorial Day weekend meant spending time with her friends, and Noura was less than enthused about Florida. She dreaded days in the car with her mom and dealing with her mom's snooty sisters. All that family stuff just bored the hell out of her. Meanwhile, her friends would be having a good time in Memphis. They were even having a party at her house! Noura now wondered why, with her mom so worked up, she had let Perry talk her into that? Her mom would blow up if she found out and Noura would never hear the end of it. Damn, Perry! He could talk her into anything.

On Friday, May 27, Noura, her mother, and her uncle Eric, left Memphis early. They drove a white minivan, one of many vehicles previously owned by Nazmi. Jennifer's effort to resolve Nazmi's estate that included two white minivans, a gray Mercedes, a black Lincoln limousine, and an older model white limousine was an ongoing difficulty. The white minivan was the only vehicle with a clear title. Jennifer had put it her name, though technically it belonged to Noura. Nazmi's death had introduced protracted arguments between mother and daughter about Noura's inheritance upon turning eighteen.

With Jennifer in the passenger seat, and Noura in back, Eric drove the full press, fourteen-hour drive to the Jackson family reunion in Orlando. The tension that had been building while loading the luggage now fully erupted inside the vehicle. Jennifer had the results of Noura's most recent drug test. "Drugs were found your system, Noura," she said. Noura's obligatory denial was met with exasperated disbelief.

"We'll deal with it when we get back to Memphis," Jennifer said. Most likely the test results confirmed the use of substances more serious than pot. Little wonder she was determined to crack down on Noura's behavior. Noura, pissed off about the drug testing and her suddenly conscripted life, was sullen. She passed her time listening to her iPod or sleeping. Please, she thought, help me be oblivious to this entire weekend.

All the uprooting and moves hadn't helped Noura's behavior. During her formative years, Noura and Jennifer moved to Arkansas, Georgia, and in and out of various homes around Memphis. Jennifer felt guilty that her personal choices impacted her daughter's life. That's one reason she spoiled her. No wonder, she thought, Noura romanticized her father. Noura made no attempt to hide her contempt for Mark, and as for the other men in Jennifer's life, she was unimpressed.

Lately Jennifer's life was a pendulum, swinging from better to worse. Her work as a bond trader was going well. She felt she was gaining control over certain aspects of her life—her job, her home. She was more realistic about Mark and their future. Or at least a little more realistic. Yet she could not control her daughter. She knew those early years full of difficulties and mistakes couldn't be undone. Maybe Noura's teenage revolt was her way of dragging the past into the present.

Like her daughter, Jennifer approached the Florida trip with trepidation. She knew two days in the car with Noura would not be easy. Not much of the last five years with Noura had been easy. Teenage moodiness, alienation and tantrums were the norm for her daughter. Jennifer accepted a lot of the blame for Noura's insecurity and unrest. Their life had been anything but calm and steady. It was so hard being a single mother—there was never that second voice of reason to back you up. Jennifer felt remorse for her inconsistent parenting. Was consistent parenting possible?

Every curfew was a battle to be won or lost. Noura seemed to flaunt the very friends Jennifer discouraged. Noura's dysfunctional relationship with Perry was so evident. They were practically a mirror of Mark and her. Off and on, harmonious one day and volatile the next.

Surely, though, Noura was a more difficult adolescent than most. Jennifer knew others saw it too. Her coworker and friend, Amy Allen, at MCI in Atlanta noted the tension back in 1999 when Noura was twelve years old. "Noura just made the relationship difficult. She made it impossible," Allen told *Commercial Appeal* reporter Stephen D. Price.

Most recently Jennifer confided in fellow bond trader Linda Finlay. There were very few women in that field, and they had grown close. Jennifer often called Linda with concerns about Noura. "It was a stormy relationship," Linda said. "Jennifer tried everything to get Noura away from bad influences."

Jennifer remembered when Patti Masterson, a friend of more than ten years, called to explain why she and her two girls had become distant. Noura and Patti's youngest daughter met in the third grade, and Patti had been an important presence in their lives. She was Jennifer's real estate agent when she bought the house in Memphis on New Haven. Both single parents, the women socialized together, sometimes even celebrated New Year's Eve.

Patti told Jennifer she was concerned about Noura's influence on her daughters. That was awful. Jennifer remembered feeling stung by her friend's words. "As the girls grew up . . . well, it was a hard conversation to have with Jennifer," Patti said.

Motherhood was a mystery to Jennifer. She thought of Noura's fondness for Dana Fredrick. My God, she practically lived with her and her daughters! And Ansley Larsson, the mother of Noura's early boyfriend, Max. Those women connected with Noura in a way she never had. Perhaps her attempts to befriend her daughter had been the wrong approach. Would the leisure of regret be hers, she wondered?

Jennifer was at the breaking point. For years things had been out of control. Now, she had an eighteen-year-old daughter—still a high school junior!—about to be thrown out of yet another school. She knew for a fact Noura was using serious drugs. But worse than that was Noura's rage. Noura wanted what she wanted, and that was all there was to it.

Jennifer was grateful her sister, Cindy Eidsen, had agreed to talk to Noura this weekend. She knew it was a lot to ask. But Cindy recognized that Jennifer needed help. They'd had so many conversations about what she was up against.

Against all odds and her better instincts, Jennifer still hoped for a meaningful vacation with her daughter. All the signals indicated otherwise.

The conflict over the drug test coincided with Eric's twenty-ninth birthday, and his memory was vivid. Jennifer held the party at her house on May 21, 2005, and Noura arrived late, looking stoned. Angry and disappointed, Jennifer confronted her daughter.

"Noura, I'm going to do a drug test on you now," she threatened. "Your eyes are red and you look high. I've been through this with you before." Jennifer knew Noura smoked pot. She'd caught Noura in the act once with Kaole by the pool, and even joked with Noura's friends about them having the munchies. Now she feared Noura's drug use had intensified and involved other, more serious drugs.

Noura quickly assured her mother she was wrong.

The party resumed though the bitter confrontation lingered, as did Jennifer's promise to drug test her daughter.

Now, en route, the results of the drug test settled heavily on the three passengers. Suspicions confirmed. Like the scene at Eric's party, Jennifer settled on a low-conflict approach, not dismissing the issue but delaying it. Jennifer knew her sister was planning to talk to Noura. In the past, Cindy and Noura had been close, though less so in Noura's teenage years. Still, she thought Noura might listen to her aunt, not shut her out the way she shut Jennifer out. This was a significant motive for the trip to Florida. Jennifer hoped that this discussion would turn the tide.

On the Saturday after the family reunion in Orlando, Jennifer, Noura, and Cindy made the four-hour drive to the Eidsen family home in Winter Park, Florida. The Jackson sisters—Jennifer, Cindy, and Grace—had a striking family resemblance to each other. All three women were tall, slender with blonde hair and lovely features—Bergdorf Blondes. The sisters appeared close and had weathered rifts and fractures made and mended. "I loved my sister completely and wholly, and I was there for her," Grace said. "I talked with her once or twice a week."

It is easy to imagine Noura feeling outside the family paradigm; sensitive to being distinctly different. Her Lebanese descent was always a prominent reminder of a rushed and unhappy marriage to a man Grace openly admitted the family "did not care for." Perhaps subconsciously Noura wasn't, as her aunt Grace said, a family person, because she truly was more comfortable with her friends and felt more of a connection.

In temperament as much as looks, Noura was nothing like her mother or her aunts. Her expressive dark eyes were alluring and often there was the play of a smile about her mouth. Her hair, though highlighted, was a dark mocha hue. Jennifer was pretty in a conventional way, but Noura's features were exotic. A triathlete with a tall stature, Jennifer was six or seven inches taller than her daughter. By contrast, Noura struggled with her weight and was self-conscious about it. Most of Noura's girlfriends were nicely proportioned, and the inevitable comparisons arose. (Someone commented that Noura was overweight and had never quite lived up to her mother's expectations, and that Jennifer once told Noura to "quit eating like a truck driver.")

Now Noura was headed to her aunt's house, trapped in a vehicle while her mother recited a litany of her offenses.

Offenses that Cindy later recalled Noura neither objected to nor challenged. Clearly, Jennifer was anxious—desperate even—to talk to Cindy about her problems with Noura that would reassert themselves so vigorously when they returned to Memphis.

Cindy said her sister was very concerned about Noura's drug use. "Jennifer," Cindy said, "had had it with her."

Jennifer wanted Noura to go to boarding school. She was eighteen years old and hadn't even finished eleventh grade! Jennifer wanted her to make new friends and change her life.

Noura had nearly been kicked out of her last school. St. George's Independent School had sent a letter home informing Jennifer that Noura had one more chance. Even Gateway wasn't working out because Noura wouldn't complete the required workbooks or tests. "Noura wouldn't even take the Gateway tests on Saturday," Cindy said. During the four-hour ride Noura offered no explanations for her behavior just as she refused to directly answer any of her mother's questions.

While none of this was news to Cindy—"I had a lot of conversations with Jennifer about the problems she was having with Noura"—it was the first time her sister asked her directly to intervene. "We were really thinking Noura could turn things around going to boarding school," Cindy said, though "Noura didn't really have much of a response to the idea."

Cindy made good on her promise to Jennifer and talked to Noura late into the night. "She listened to me—I was surprised by that—she didn't shut me out." But she was noncommittal. Then a phone call from Memphis shut down any hope of progress. Before leaving town Jennifer had asked her across-the-street neighbor, Joe Cocke, to keep an eye on her house. Saturday night he called to report a full-blown pool party was underway.

Jennifer and Noura lived directly across the street from Sheila Cocke and her husband for years. In 2004, Mr. Cocke's health deteriorated, and their son Joe and his wife Rachael moved in to help with his care. Joe and Rachael eventually bought the home at 5000 New Haven from his mother who still lived with them. Joe owned a landscaping and lawn care business, and weekly serviced Jennifer's yard. But until the morning of June 5, 2005, Joe would later testify, he had never been inside the house.[1]

The Cocke family contributed some of the trial's most explosive and sensational testimony. Joe and Rachael related the terror of the early morning hours of June. They also were positive they did not see the wicker basket that morning—the two-foot-long, brown basket that was turned open side down to cover Jennifer's face, head, and neck—that the first medical responder and Noura described.

In her witness statement, Noura recounted finding her mother. Moments later she ran across the street to the Cockes' residence:

> So I walked into my mom's room and I took the basket off her head. I tried to talk to her, but she wouldn't talk, then I tried to feel pulse, I

[1] Some of Noura's supporters following her trial disputed Joe Cocke's claim that he previously had not been inside the home.

> kept shaking her, then I ran out the front door to the neighbor's house and got them and I was screaming and they followed me back and then I ran into the sun room to call the cops from the land phone and then I went in the kitchen and sat on the floor and I was holding my cat screaming just waiting for them to get there.

When Joe told Jennifer he would look after her house Memorial Day weekend, trouble seemed unlikely. Noura was with her mom, which made the prospect of a party doubtful, or so he thought until teenagers began rolling in Saturday night.

"Kids just started showing up. . . . There must have been forty to fifty kids. They came with their brown bags and their beer bottles, and went into the backyard," Cocke said. The block Joe and Jennifer shared is a small one with a dead end. Cocke said because of that neighbors noticed traffic, and normally when Noura's friends visited her, they parked at the end of the street and walked to her home. Saturday night they pulled directly up in front of the house, knowing, he surmised, Jennifer was gone.

Growing concerned, he turned the lights off in his kitchen to better observe the arrivals. The teenagers headed for the backyard to gather around the pool. Joe and Rachael discussed whether or not to call Jennifer and finally agreed it would be best. The next call was to the Memphis police. The partygoers started jumping the fence, "going every which-a-way," Joe said, and ran across

Mendenhall—a busy Memphis street—as the police tried to get in the backyard.

The backyard fence gate was tricky, Joe knew that from mowing the Jackson lawn, and the time it took police to open it was just enough for the teenagers to make their escape. When the police left, the kids briefly returned, jumping back over the fence.

Jennifer had asked Noura's boyfriend Perry to feed Boo, the family's dog, and water the plants while they were away. And she gave him a house key. Instead of looking after the property, he was the party's ringleader. He filled Noura in on his plans in advance, promising that just a few people would be over. Perry admitted the party got out of hand.

A quiet afternoon by the pool with a few friends and some beer grew into quite a large group by nightfall. Perry said when the police arrived he had hidden in the backyard but eventually realized he would have to talk with them. He was relieved not to have been arrested.

Kaole remembered Memorial Day weekend at Noura's as initially casual. Folks were sitting around the backyard drinking and smoking pot until the police showed up. "Everybody smoked," he said, "unless your school drug tested. And some who went to those schools didn't care." Like Perry, Kaole was not eager to speak with the police. He jumped the fence and crouched in the neighbor's bushes until the place cleared out again.

Perry knew there would be repercussions. Tension was high between Noura and him and also, he knew, between Jennifer and Noura. For the first time he could recall, Noura was in trouble with her mom over drugs. If Jennifer had let things slide in the past, she appeared to have no intention of doing so anymore.

Given the opportunity, most teenagers will throw a party when favorable conditions exist, like the absence of parents. Noura's situation was a little more interesting. She wasn't even home to enjoy the party but granted such liberty to her friends, and Perry in particular.

When Jennifer received the call between 6:00 and 7:00 p.m. that Saturday night at her sister's home in Winter Park, Florida, she was furious. Joe told Jennifer that a lot of people had shown up at her home, and a "wild party" was underway. Jennifer immediately confronted her daughter "Are you having another party at our house?" There'd been a party there six months earlier, and Jennifer was outraged it was happening again. Noura denied any knowledge of the party.

That Saturday night in Florida was anything but a party. Jennifer was at the end of her rope with her daughter, and Noura acted the wounded outsider, refusing any part of the family gathering. "I don't know what to do," Jennifer repeated with even more exasperation. "You're eighteen years old. You'll have to go to boarding school or into the military." Noura volleyed back that she'd join the military.

The next morning Perry called Jennifer to apologize about the party. He knew she would find out and thought it better to let her know he was sorry. Armed with Perry's confirmation, she confronted Noura, who finally admitted she had known all along. Offering, "yes, I did, sorry," Noura promised it wouldn't happen again.

Cindy described the rest of the weekend as uncomfortable. Mother and daughter heatedly argued downstairs, shouting back and forth about "the party Noura had organized at her house." Then they "took it upstairs," where the feud raged on another thirty minutes. When they returned downstairs, "Noura was sullen and wouldn't look anyone in the eye." She was obviously upset and angry. Cindy also observed that Noura looked sad.

There was no escaping Sunday's hostile climate. "Jennifer and Noura wouldn't talk to each other. It was very cold," Cindy said. Noura broke the silence by asking Eric about the military. "Noura said she'd go into the military," Eric recalled. "And I said, 'If you can't abide by your mother's rules, what makes you think you can abide by military rules?'" Eric made it clear to Noura that she certainly didn't need to go off joining the military. Discussion of Noura's future "pretty much ended there."

The military? Boarding school? Noura couldn't decide which one she found more fucking hilarious. She saw herself with a bunch of immature sixteen and seventeen-year-old girls wearing the standard plaid jumper of most girls' schools. Noura imagined the scene—no one she could possibly relate to, and she'd probably be the oldest student there! She laughed remembering Aunt Cindy's sincerity and encouragement. It was funny. What was her mom thinking? Noura would never survive in the military, with its rules and restrictions. When had that ever worked for her?

A surprise lately for Noura was her uncle Eric. Noura remembered times when they had partied together. He had been cool and fun. What happened to him? Now he acted so straight and mature. She missed being able to trust him.

He had lived with Noura and Jennifer for a few years. And even when he had his own place, he had dinner with them a lot and hung out. But lately he aligned with her mom against her.

Once while helping Jennifer clear dishes out of Noura's room, he called her room a "pigsty"—not true!—and then pointed out a box of condoms—"big box of blue condoms"—on Noura's dresser. That was none of his business! Noura couldn't wait to get home and see her friends. This trip had been even worse than she had imagined.

Early Monday morning with Eric at the wheel they left Florida for Memphis. Relations between mother and daughter thawed a little during the fourteen-hour drive home. Jennifer took a business call that was typical for her. Even Noura's friends noticed Jennifer's work ethic. Sophie said, "Her mom worked all the time." So a business call on vacation was not out of the ordinary. What *was* unusual was that the call prompted Noura to ask her mom questions about bonds. How do bonds work? How many bonds could Jennifer sell? How much money could Jennifer make off of one bond?

That led to a discussion of Jennifer's 401k and her life insurance policy. Jennifer assured Noura that she would be well taken care of should anything happen to her. Jennifer's estate was valued at almost $1.5 million in securities and personal property. An indication of Jennifer's success at thirty-nine years of age. Jennifer said Noura was on both policies, and Eric was on her 401k. The conversation about Jennifer's financial plans continued for a while, helping to lift the mood. They stopped to shop a little—at some point during this trip Jennifer bought Noura a pair of gray New Balance tennis shoes—and by Eric's account the trip was "normal."

Growing Up Noura

"Noura would knock on her mother's door when they were through, through with 'the act.'"—Family friend

Even the most optimistic matchmaker probably would have passed on pairing Nazmi Chafic Hassanieh with Jennifer Schroeder Jackson. But once Nazmi met Jennifer—both were undergraduates at Memphis State University and worked at The Peabody hotel—he was determined to date the tall, beautiful blonde. Jennifer's appearance would have complemented the heavily ornate and opulent hotel, a landmark in Downtown Memphis since 1925. Author David Cohn said of the South's Grand Hotel, "The Mississippi Delta begins in the lobby of the Peabody Hotel and ends on Catfish Row in Vicksburg," a quotation often attributed to William Faulkner. The Peabody's lobby displays enormous arrangements of fresh flowers; a travertine marble fountain from Italy that is occupied by five pampered ducks; a distinguished duck master who cares for the mallards; a grand piano and pianist; and a bustling and sophisticated bar. Nazmi would not have fit in at The Peabody as easily as Jennifer. He didn't sport her movie-star looks. He was a short man, 5'5," and a Lebanese foreign national, but those differences did not deter him from pursuing her.

Nazmi's friend of twenty years, Gloria Hodge, described him as "the life of the party. He was a handsome man in the face with an outgoing personality. A charming man." Gloria and Nazmi met when they worked in the same building and he later moved into the apartment complex where Gloria lived.

It must have been Nazmi's charm that attracted Jennifer and led to the eventual courtship. It was hard for some to see them as a couple, especially given their disparate heights and backgrounds. Nazmi also was four years older than Jennifer. He was born January 1, 1961, in Lebanon, and she was born in Savannah, Georgia, November 10, 1965.

Jennifer's pregnancy no doubt hastened the seriousness of their relationship. On December 13, 1986, they married at St. Mary's Episcopal Cathedral in Memphis. Noura Hodo Nazmi Hassanieh was born just three months later on St. Patrick's Day, March 17, 1987. (Hodo was Nazmi's mother's name, but Jennifer later changed Noura's middle name to Grace after her sister.) If Jennifer was looking for an anchor after a difficult childhood—her father died and her mother was an alcoholic—her tumultuous marriage to Nazmi was certainly not that.

Divorce is always wrenching, but Jennifer's parents' breakup tore the very fabric of the family. When Linda and Bo Jackson split up, Linda appeared to leave more than her husband. Those close said she also abandoned her three daughters. And when she eventually remarried, the girls did not want to live in Orlando, Florida, with her and their stepfather, Larry Sherwood, even though they had a new half brother as well. Eric Sherwood was born in 1976. Instead, the three teenagers moved in 1980 to Memphis to live with their uncle and aunt, The Reverend and Mrs. C.E. Reeves, Jr. Jennifer was fifteen years old at the time.

Linda's struggle with alcohol was the root of the family's dysfunction. Eventually she and Sherwood divorced, and Linda was awarded custody of Eric. This arrangement was short lived. After Linda caused a fire in their apartment, Eric's custody was awarded to his father, Larry, and his new wife.

Despite the displacement and chaos of those years, Jennifer remained a bright star. She finished high school in three years and college in three years, and essentially took care of herself from the time she was seventeen years old.

Split families, half siblings, and sets of relatives "once removed," practically have become the cultural norm. In that regard, the Jackson and Sherwood families are not alone. Over the years Noura did get to know her maternal grandmother, but Jennifer and her sisters remained largely estranged from their mother, and the sisters themselves did not seem especially close. Eric, however, had on occasion lived with Jennifer, and she helped and cared for him when possible.

Renae McMillan, who formerly was married to Eric, said she had known the Memphis branch of the Jackson family for nine years but had never met Grace or Cindy. According to Renae, "They had no relationship with Jennifer." Renae's perspective certainly contradicted Cindy and Grace's characterization of their relationship with their sister at Noura's murder trial.

If she had been too hasty to marry, Jennifer realized her mistake just as quickly. (Nazmi's friend Gloria said the couple's relationship faltered when Jennifer's mother moved in with them for a while.) Jennifer filed for divorce September 9, 1987, when Noura was six months old. But in December of that same year she allowed Nazmi to move back into her apartment. She regretted the decision almost immediately. She repeatedly asked him to leave, and in May of 1988 a physical altercation occurred. Nazmi knocked her to the ground. Jennifer filed court papers stating he had beaten her and threatened to kill both her and Noura. She further stated she feared Nazmi would take Noura out of the country.

Nazmi was ordered to leave the apartment, and Jennifer was granted temporary custody of Noura. Nazmi claimed in divorce proceedings that Jennifer, like her mother, was not maternal. He stated that Linda deserted her three daughters three weeks after she divorced their father. He even provided the names of Linda Jackson Sherwood and Cindy Jackson as witnesses to prove his point that Jennifer was not a fit mother. However, his efforts for custody did not prevail, and in November of 1988 Jennifer was granted full custody.

In 1992, Jennifer changed Noura's name to Noura Grace Jackson. Jennifer might have thought this simple solution would further remove Nazmi from their lives. By anglicizing Noura's middle name, did she hope to sever Noura's ties to her father's culture as well? Though she was only five years old when her mother changed her name, as Noura got older she told her friends she did not mind the name change. "Noura Grace Jackson" lacked the cumbersome spelling and inevitable questions "Noura Hodo Nazmi Hassanieh" evoked.

What the final divorce didn't accomplish was an end to parental bickering. They continued to argue in and out of court for years, often over delinquent child support payments. Gloria recalled that Nazmi's weekend visitations with Noura were a further source of conflict with Jennifer. But despite such obstacles, Gloria considered Noura and her father to be very close. "Nazmi and Jennifer argued fairly consistently," Gloria said. "He would spoil Noura—buy her clothes, gifts—and that would anger Jennifer." Gloria admitted Nazmi had "worries," but that for him, "Jennifer was always a problem."

Nazmi was eerily present at 5001 New Haven the morning of June 5. As he first appraised the crime scene, Homicide Detective Tim Helldorfer noticed a TV in the kitchen and, for no real reason, turned it on. "There was something kind of strange that morning when I was in the house. There's a TV in the kitchen. Just for the heck of it I turned it on. Pushed the play button. There was a videotape of Noura and her dad when Noura is about three years old. And she had a knife in her hand and was playing with it, and her dad was saying, 'You have to be careful with knives, someone can get hurt.'"

Jennifer, now twenty-three years old, was officially a single mother. Naturally she had romances. According to a family friend, as a toddler Noura learned "not to come in her mother's room until her mommy quit making noises." One relationship from these early years involved William "Bill" Shelton, who later returned to Noura's life in a surprising manner much as her own father had. Shelton and Jennifer dated when Noura was a toddler. Depending on the source, Shelton was Jennifer's friend, boyfriend, or one-time fiancé. "Jennifer," according to her sister, Grace, "described [the relationship] more as a close friendship. Maybe it was different to him."

Whatever his relationship was to Jennifer, Shelton cared deeply for her young daughter. After Jennifer and Shelton broke up, he sought ways to see Noura and eventually found a conduit through Nazmi. He visited Noura at Nazmi's when she stayed with her father. When Noura turned eighteen, Shelton contacted her, suggesting a visit.

Jennifer married Jimmy Harris, Jr., an Arkansas farmer, on December 23, 1992, the same year she changed Noura's name. She and five-year-old Noura moved to Arkansas. A new home, a new town, a new father, and a new school; thus began another chapter in Noura's nomadic life. In less than three years the mother and daughter would make six moves. In Memphis, Noura had been attending private schools, St. Mary's Episcopal School and later Lausanne Collegiate School. These schools had solid reputations, and it is hard to imagine that the transition to a different school advanced her academic performance.

Jennifer's luck with men didn't improve with Jimmy Harris. Twenty-seven years old when she married him and not quite thirty when they separated, the marriage was fraught with transgressions. Harris was a gambler and a philanderer. According to divorce records, in a gambling spree in Tunica, Mississippi, Harris lost $45,000 in a two-week period; and between September 1995 and January 1996, also in Tunica, he lost another $100,000. For four months Eric lived with the couple and Noura in their Arkansas home. To Eric, the marriage was strange. "Jim," he said, "stayed gone all day and most of the night. [He] usually came home around midnight."

His sister told him Harris cheated on her. Divorce papers state that Harris admitted his infidelity and he said that Jennifer knew the identity of the other woman. Worse for Jennifer was the case of herpes he gave her. For that he paid Jennifer's medical treatment as well as $180.00 a month in counseling fees. Hardly restitution enough for the abuse she endured. The divorce records indicate that Harris assaulted Jennifer in front of Noura. Jennifer now had two abusive marriages to her credit—both witnessed by her young daughter.

Their marriage's volatility spilled over into the divorce proceedings. During a May 1996 deposition, Harris pulled a loaded gun and pointed it at Jennifer's attorney, R. Sadler Bailey. Jennifer later calmly related this story to her brother.

Yet for all the sound and fury of their divorce attempt, it remained unresolved for a number of years.

Noura and Jennifer, who was still legally married to Harris, moved for a time to Atlanta, Georgia, where she worked for MCI. In Atlanta, Jennifer struck up a friendship with coworker Amy Allen. Allen was someone Jennifer confided in about Noura's burgeoning rebelliousness.

When Jennifer refiled for divorce in September 2001, the proceedings went smoothly, and the divorce was final by October 2001. Jennifer waived alimony and restored her name to Jennifer Schroeder Jackson.

She'd always been a hard worker. She was a successful insurance agent for Allstate and Farmers before her career in investment banking blossomed. The New Haven house was in Jennifer's name and clear except for taxes. Owning her home may have given her a certain security about the future. Jennifer and Noura's years in the East Memphis home were as settled a period as they'd known. Though no one would have imagined that 5001 New Haven would be Jennifer's last residence.

Free Kitten

"We stopped and got a free kitten.
A little, free kitten."—Kaole

"Is it possible that a cat could move evidence,
smear wet blood? That the cat could have been
on Jennifer's bed and moved blood elsewhere?"
Defense attorney Corder to Officer David Payment

"A cat may have moved—may have digested—
evidence,"—Payment concurred upon viewing the image
of the cat in a crime-scene photograph of the kitchen.

When Noura and Kaole took Alex to the new house where she lived with her dad, Noura ran in to borrow a hair dryer even though she undoubtedly had any number at her own house. That summer when most of Noura's friends were rising seniors, there was ample time to relax by the pool, party, and concentrate on appearances. Somehow the girls managed to defy Memphis humidity. They kept their hair long and smooth. The frequent outfit changes meant traveling with Vera Bradley bags. Many seemed relatively relaxed about curfews and family rule; and until recently, Noura had been among the most nonchalant. Her friend Kirby said, "Noura didn't really have a curfew."

As she and Kaole neared her house, Noura was disappointed to see her mom's car still in the driveway. What's taking her so long, she wondered! She was eager to take a shower and start getting ready. They already had been to Eastgate to check parking and buy beer. What could they do to kill some time until her mom left? Noura remembered the sign for the free kittens. She and Kaole drove over and went inside. Noura was an animal lover and couldn't resist the adorable bundle of kittens. She chose a small black one. "A little, free kitten," Kaole said.

As Noura and Kaole pulled away with the kitten, the couple looked at each other and wondered if they'd done the right thing. They talked about how young the kids were. Almost everyone likes a kitten, but would the girl really give it a good home? Those teenagers had looked messed up. Like they'd had a long day in the sun and a few beers. He had some of the wildest, blond curly hair they'd ever seen. And the kitty seemed like a spur of the moment idea to the girl. Well, they'd assured her she could bring him back if it didn't work out, especially since her mom had no idea her daughter was bringing a pet home. Probably a mistake, they realized, but done.

As they approached Noura's home, they could see all was clear. There was nothing ostentatious about the Jackson residence, and compared to the neighborhood houses, it was a poor relation. Its understated earth tones and minimal landscaping suggested indifference, if not neglect. The front entrance, protected by a wood portico, amounted to no more than two brick steps and an iron security door over a wooden door that opened into a modest foyer.

The foyer essentially divided the house into two parts. To the right were the primary common living areas: a kitchen on the front with windows facing the street, New Haven; the living and dining room areas; and a step down to the sunroom.

The sunroom faced the backyard and swimming pool with its own exterior entrance, a wood door and a security door. The sunroom doors opened onto a shaded, ill-kept, covered walkway. Turn right, and you see a door to the garage. Turn left, and you're in the backyard.

The kitchen had its own door—a wood door with three horizontal panes of glass and a hidden, hinge lock near the middle pane of glass—which offered immediate access to the garage. A handy feature for unloading groceries.

Off the foyer to the left was a long, dimly lit hallway. The first door on the left side of the hall was a common bathroom. Farther down the hall on the left was Jennifer's bedroom and private bathroom, a corner room on the front of the house. Straight across the hall from Jennifer's room was Noura's bedroom. The other room on right side of the hallway—across from the shared bathroom and closer to the foyer—was a maroon and pink bedroom converted into a large closet.

While he waited for Noura to shower and dress, Kaole played with the kitty; had a couple of beers; and noticed Jennifer's new set of Callaway golf clubs. He was a golf caddy at Germantown Country Club and recognized it was a nice set. A random pitching wedge in the kitchen escaped his notice however. It actually belonged to Jennifer's boyfriend, Mark Irwin. Kaole had heard Noura say a few choice words about Irwin! Kaole swung one of the clubs he'd admired—a Callaway with a fiberglass shaft—around inside and outside of the house. As a caddy he was in the habit of putting a club back in its proper place, so he dipped the club in the pool, cleaned it off, and put it precisely back in the bag.

Noura endured the usual travails of picking out clothes. Knowing Perry would be there made her more attentive to what she wore and how she looked. Technically they weren't together, but maybe that would change tonight. Thankfully her hair and nails were pretty much done. Her French manicure was still pristine. And as she looked in the mirror, she saw how much sun she'd gotten that afternoon.

Tonight she eventually settled on a white flowy skirt that came just below the knee. She wore a yellow top with white embroidered flowers and narrow straps. Her shoes, shiny, gold sandals with rhinestones, were new. She'd only had them a couple of weeks. The top and skirt she'd stolen. Stupid risk-taking, she knew, but easily accomplished. And she'd avoid her mom's usual line of questioning: where did you get it, how much did it cost, and so on. If only her mood was light as her outfit! The bickering with her mom and breakup with Perry dulled her prospects of a good time. Plus, she felt like she was getting her period, some slight cramping now that she knew would get worse. Noura had such a difficult time with menstrual cramps that her doctor prescribed Lortab. Usually the doctor didn't prescribe enough but she would augment the prescription by buying more on the street. She discovered she could make money buying and selling Lortab. When her uncle told her she needed a job to keep herself occupied she told him that "she'd just go into business selling pills." He had nothing to say to that.

A few weeks ago she'd called her mom at work with perfectly reasonable requests. The conversation was pleasant enough for a while but quickly soured when Noura said she needed a haircut and color and $150.00 for a pair of jeans she'd found. That was nothing compared to the way her mom spent money! Their house was literally exploding with stuff! Sometimes Noura couldn't believe how Jennifer bought duplicates or more of the same crap. Clothes that would never be worn. The garage and storage areas were full. So was the spare bedroom. It was crazy to live that way and such bullshit for her mom to get on *her* about spending money! Jennifer balked about any money Noura asked for, even essentials like her hair appointment. Her mom thought the salon she liked was too expensive. So ridiculous. More and more she told her no. It especially was maddening because by now she shouldn't have to be asking for money. *She* should be controlling her dad's estate not her mom.

Best not to go down that road. Noura knew her mood would darken even more if those thoughts persisted. Tonight was supposed to be one of the best parties of the summer. It would start off with the girls getting ready—changing clothes, smoking a little, drinking. Noura thought of her girlfriends, and she felt things were easier for them. How did they manage to stay so impossibly thin? They didn't even try. She had to struggle with her weight and argue with her mom over everything she wanted. And some of them could be such brats! Noura thought of the stupid fights she and Kirby had and how they wouldn't speak for weeks. Going out tonight was starting to feel like too much trouble. She couldn't shake her bitter feelings. Somehow she needed to mellow out, maybe take a few Lortabs.

Dressed and ready, Noura walked into the living room to find Kaole relaxing. They'd smoked some at his house earlier while he was getting ready, and now he was kicked back on the couch. Just as they were leaving, Kaole asked Noura for a glass of water to get rid of his cotton mouth. He left the glass on the kitchen counter.

Just the Girls

"No one was feuding at Carter's house. We sat on a porch off a bedroom and smoked. We talked about mothers and how nice Noura's mom always was to us. Noura said, 'My mom's a bitch and she needs to go to hell.'"—Kirby McDonald

It wasn't long before Carter Kobeck's house filled up with the regulars. However, one important person was missing. Carter was out of town with his family. Still, as Noura had Memorial Day weekend, he made his friends welcome in his parents' home for the second pre-Italian Fest party. Around seven or seven-thirty Kirby pulled up with Sophie and Brooke Thompson. Noura and Kaole arrived a little later in her Jeep. One thing Brooke remembered about that night was that almost everyone was getting along.

Like any group of friends, there were varying degrees of attachments and loyalties; but despite waxing and waning affections, their recent grief united them. They were mourning a vital member. Anna's death in January, a mere six months before, introduced the teenagers to mortality and the searing pain of loss. Anna had been the group's linchpin—she was the medium for many of their introductions and eventual friendships—and her absence haunted them.

The paths of the four girls gathered tonight had zigzagged as they moved in and out of various schools: Immaculate Conception, St. Agnes, and Ridgeway. Sophie and Noura knew each other in grade school, having played basketball together at Jennifer and Noura's church, Church of the Holy Communion, in East Memphis. They were separated at the end of Sophie's sophomore year when she moved to Dallas. But on her visits home they would get together—mostly going to house parties at the time. By the end of Sophie's junior year she had returned to Memphis, and her time with Noura was more consistent. They probably would be together a couple of times a week. "A lot of the time when we were out at night we were all doing drugs, drinking," Sophie said. "Everyone was doing it." Noura's house, in particular out by the pool, was a spot they favored.

Brooke and Noura met in 2000 in the seventh grade at St. Agnes. That also was the year Noura met Anna. Anna became not only her dear friend but also someone who enhanced Noura's circle. Anna's many contacts bridged a number of schools, and they became Noura's as well. Anna in fact introduced Noura to Kirby. A friendship that proved difficult as the two girls formed a habit of sparring and reconciling. Kirby admitted she fought with Noura more than her other friends. Surely one source of friction was Perry. He dated Kirby as well as Noura, and that led to hard feelings. A few months before Anna died, Noura and Kirby were not even speaking. Though after the tragedy, Kirby said they made up.

The girls didn't linger long in the kitchen but moved instead to Carter's sister's bedroom to get ready together. They sat for awhile on the bed. Sophie, seated to Noura's left, noticed when Noura took three Lortabs.[2] That was something she'd seen Noura do before, so she didn't think much of it.

They were roused when friend, Clark Schifani, wandered into the bedroom. He recorded this rare moment of harmony by snapping their picture with Brooke's cell phone. (The girls most likely didn't give a passing thought to this photo, yet it garnered the spotlight at Noura's trial for its evidence of Noura's first outfit that night.) Sophie, Brooke, and Kirby, individually and collectively, composed a striking trio, with summer tans and youthful radiance. Sophie and Brooke were tall and blonde, while Kirby, a beautiful brunette, was closer to Noura's height. Arms intertwined, Noura stood at one end beside Brooke, then Sophie, with Kirby at the other end. The girls wore sleeveless or strapless tops revealing ample cleavage. Noura looked out of place in the spontaneous photo. While Brooke, Sophie, and Kirby smiled broadly for Clark, warmly beckoning the camera, Noura stood stolidly. Her yellow top gathered unflatteringly just under her bust line making her appear heavier than her friends. Her flat facial expression heightened the effect. "I don't think Noura felt she was like the other girls," a

---

[2] Far from making someone energetic and animated, Lortab—a combination of the narcotic pain reliever hydrocodone and acetaminophen—generally has the opposite effect, producing a quiet, lulling feeling. There also are individuals who attest to Lortab making them sleepless, jittery, and anxious, even causing strange, unusual thoughts and hallucinations. Taken long enough and frequently enough, Lortab's effectiveness as a pain reliever can be diminished. It also poses the risk of addiction.

juror from Noura's trial remarked. "She didn't smile like the other girls."

When Clark rejoined the group in the kitchen, the female foursome moved to the porch off the bedroom to smoke. As she had dreaded, Noura couldn't shake her dour mood and it was evident to the others. Noura, who was often the life of the party, "loud and the center of conversation, just sat there," according to Sophie. "Noura was quieter than usual," Sophie recalled. "Very quiet and reserved."

Kirby remembered Noura brightened a bit when she showed off her new manicure. "She said 'I just got a manicure' and showed the girls her nails. It was a French manicure with white powder to make your actual nails look longer." Kirby grabbed Noura's hands to look closer at the manicure, acrylic French with white tips.

Noura wasn't the only one using drugs heavier than marijuana that night. Kirby had taken one-fourth of a Xanax bar along with her Bud Light. "Just the smallest amount of the bar because I was driving," she testified. She had never taken a Xanax bar before and wanted to see what it was like. Her self-professed moderation later came into question. After Noura's arrest, Kirby, according to defense attorney Art Quinn, confided to a friend "To tell you the truth, I was so fucked up that night I don't know what happened."

Noura lit another cigarette and sank back in the chair. She looked around and made the usual comparisons. They were all slimmer, prettier, richer, and happier than she was. Again she felt the piercing void of Anna's absence. Anna was her true friend, her real friend. Anna made her feel good about herself. Together they were adventuresome. Noura remembered when they snorted cocaine together in the ninth grade. Sophie was with them too. They were in a car in front of Noura's house. Sometimes she was amazed at how clueless her mom could be.

Noura looked down at her new gold sandals and suddenly determined her entire outfit was wrong. She felt stiff and ungainly. She couldn't keep her thoughts from racing ahead to seeing Perry and wondering how that would go. (How rattled Noura would have been to know Sophie and Brooke planned to ditch her later so Sophie could hook up with Perry.)

Waves of resentment washed over her. She hated feeling that way. It wasn't really her. Surely, she thought, those Lortabs will kick in soon. She must be taking them too often. It took more of them to feel any relief. Tonight she needed emotional and physical relief. The nagging cramps she'd tried to ignore were getting worse. This sort of discomfort usually meant her period would soon follow.

The others were in high spirits that Noura couldn't possibly match. Still, sitting here talking with them was easy enough. Then someone started talking about mothers. For Noura, that was an unpleasant topic. The girls went on and on about how pretty Jennifer was and how nice she was to them. Noura surprised herself when she blurted out, "My mom's a bitch and she needs to go to hell."

Ugh, she thought, that was harsh. Where did it come from? She felt relieved her outburst reached only this small cluster. She didn't want to be the angry, pouting girl. Unshaken, her friends barely acknowledged Noura's outburst. For Kirby there was nothing peculiar about it, "Just a teenager in a fight with her mom."

Mark

On June 5, 2005, his birthday, Mark Irvin awoke at 6:00 a.m., headed to McDonald's for Sunday breakfast, memorized his sermon, went to church, preached two sermons, and taught Sunday school. Outside the First United Methodist Church, a Jackson, Tennessee, police officer was waiting to speak with him. The officer delivered the news of Jennifer's death.

Jennifer hung up the phone Saturday afternoon and asked herself again why she'd called Mark. She was doing most of the calling these days; his calls to her were fewer and fewer. This last conversation amazed her. She offered to drive to Jackson, Tennessee, Sunday morning and listen to his sermon! That alone should convince him she really wanted another chance. Sunday was Mark's birthday, and she suggested a birthday dinner. She couldn't believe he flat out told her no.

"Why don't you want me to come to your church?" she asked. "Is it because you're not ready to get back with me?"

He made no denial. Jennifer didn't know if she felt more anger than disappointment. She allowed Mark to consume four years of her life and now this! Granted the years had been tempestuous—they broke up and reconciled about every five months—but those years were also, Mark later testified, "healthy and good."

His rejection of the birthday dinner brought back memories of last Christmas. She surprised him with a trip to New York as his Christmas gift. He seemed delighted, but before the trip they were out one night and got in a stupid fight over the check. That was all it took for him to say he wasn't going. Jennifer couldn't believe it. The plane ticket, all of it, refused. To her that seemed rigid and unreasonable.

After they met in 2001, her friends teased her about dating a minister. Jennifer had grown up in the care of her uncle, a minister, so Mark's profession was comfortable for her. Though they certainly weren't the perfect couple. Mark was shorter with slightly graying hair and a bit of a dandy. He drove her crazy with his talk, talk, talk. And she had nagging doubts about his sincerity. When he insisted they go to a couples' counseling weekend through his church, deep down she wondered if it was a setup—a way to make her feel like *she* was the problem. The weekend, he said, would address their "communication and control problems." Those words he used—our relationship's "growing edge." What in the hell was that?

They were both given to rash behavior and quick anger, like the fights that erupted in restaurants, or the way she abruptly left New Orleans by bus. This behavior didn't seem nearly as insurmountable to her as they did to Mark. Jennifer knew too well from her two marriages that conflict always was part of it. Mark was in his mid-to-late forties and had never been married. She thought he had unrealistic expectations and over analyzed their bumps in the road.

He never forgave her for leaving him in New Orleans. And she still got mad thinking about it. They had been walking down Decatur Street, having a good time, and she asked a passing woman to take their photograph. The lady was happy to do so, and Jennifer suggested a good place to take the photograph. It was perfectly harmless and Mark blew it all out of proportion.

"Jennifer, you're so controlling," he told her again.

"We'll never get along," she yelled. "I'm leaving." She found the Greyhound bus station and headed back to Memphis. Typical Mark, he walked on to the restaurant, got a table, and waited for her. He was flabbergasted and outraged when she called him from the bus en route. It took a long time to get past that one. If they ever did.

And sex. What kind of grown man sleeps on top of the sheets fully dressed? That was another one of his demands. He wanted their relationship—all aspects of it—to be in the context of marriage. When that argument erupted, he'd pull the sleeping-in-his-clothes routine or head home. Or, they would play musical beds. He slept on the couch, or Jennifer slept in Noura's bed if Noura was away, just to appease him. If Noura was home, that necessitated a different protocol. They rarely had sex in that case, as he was so aware of her daughter's presence.

Jennifer preferred sleeping in the nude or in big t-shirts and found intimacy very natural. Why introduce barriers or impose rules? She even bought the condoms.

The marriage issue hovered over them. He told her he loved her and wanted to marry her. Jennifer thought that was sweet, but the realist in her knew it was too early to consider marriage. Why couldn't he just give in and enjoy what they had now?

She thought all the issues between them could be managed with more tolerance. It didn't help that Noura and Mark were water and oil. Whenever she and Mark split up, Noura was quick to tell her mom what a hypocrite Mark was, how he used his front as a minister to make people think he was nice.

Noura minced no words when it came to Mark, describing him in her witness statement to police as "a big, selfish asshole." Even Noura's eighth-grade boyfriend, Max Quinlan, had strong feelings about Mark whom he considered, according to his mom, "showy, pompous, and excessively competitive."

But Jennifer clung to the times things were right with Mark. He was a refuge from her problems with Noura. Between the two of them, she thought with exhaustion, she'd never have peace.

Jennifer and Mark had shared a good laugh when he discovered that his missing golf club—his pitching wedge—was at her house. He'd been looking for it for the past two or three months and had even been to several courses he'd played asking about it. She missed those outings—the times they played golf in beautiful weather and he was easy to get along with.

As the years passed, petty arguments more frequently consumed their time. Together, they were combustible. Disagreements, frustrations, hurt feelings usually led to one of them walking away—"fleeing" as Mark called it—though not before some heated exchanges. When Mark's temper flared Jennifer retaliated. All too often it happened in public. It seemed they had a knack for flare-ups in restaurants. A long-time Memphis waiter observed, "Disagreements are as real as leaves falling from the trees." He might well have been describing Mark and Jennifer.

She grimaced to think of their restaurant scenes. One night in Marena's, a romantic Italian restaurant in Memphis, Mark's outburst had been too much for her and the argument escalated. Their server was visibly alarmed. She couldn't remember who left first that time. (People around them later described the argument as violent.) The dining scenario that led to their most recent breakup took place in a small, Vietnamese restaurant. They were eating at Lotus where the tables are very close together. When Jennifer thought back on the night, she realized again how ill-suited the place was for the discussion that ensued. Mark wanted to talk about their future. In moments they were angry.

When she stormed out—or was it Mark?—it seemed unlikely they would talk again. But she missed him. She drove to see him in Jackson a day or two after that blowup and spent the night. She thought she could pacify him; instead he was more remote and immovable than ever. By morning he was adamant that there was no point in picking up where they had left off. He wanted to take things to the next level—marriage—and that was that.

Despite her overtures they were stuck in the post-Lotus moment. A month had passed, and other than a few phone calls, they hadn't seen each other. She was ready to drive the eighty plus miles to see him tomorrow for his birthday but was rebuffed. Maybe she should insist he return her house keys and truly make the break official.

Without the drive to Jackson tomorrow morning, Jennifer felt her weekend plans expanding. Maybe it was for the better. She had a business trip to California on Friday and plenty to do beforehand. She and Jimmy Tual were attending the Fuller wedding, and they'd probably grab a drink at one of Jennifer's favorite spots, the Cockeyed Camel, afterwards. Who cares if people joked that it was a middle-aged pick-up place? It was usually fun and relaxed.

Jimmy was a welcome relief from Mark. When she and Mark were off again, Jimmy stepped in as escort. No romance, just a solid friendship. Amazing, Jennifer thought, she'd known Jimmy seventeen years. They were each other's relationship counselor. He was an empathetic listener and a loyal friend.

She had no idea what to expect when Jimmy met Mark at a pool party at her house. She knew Mark sometimes got not-so-kind reviews. If Jimmy felt that way he never let on; his comments were almost always gentle. They helped each other out with business ideas too. Jimmy published his own real-estate magazine and Jennifer loved to pass along her ideas. But she didn't confide in him about Noura. Funny how certain friendships adapt to predictable conversation lines. She and Jimmy jogged together, and on occasion, played squash. For a while, they were part of a Calvary Episcopal dinner group. Jennifer admired his adept socializing skills and powers of persuasion. He could get her out and about even when she wasn't in the mood.

Yes, going out tonight and the trip to California on Friday looked better all the time. But as quickly as those feelings arrived, they departed. Her chest constricted with dread and anxiety. What would she do about Noura while she was out of town? My eighteen-year-old daughter, she thought with sadness and frustration, controls my life. God knows she couldn't leave her home alone after the Memorial Day weekend fiasco and asking the Cockes to help was out of the question. She'd have to convince Eric to stay with Noura. She saw no other option. Noura would be mad about Eric of course, but anger was Noura's common state these days.

Jennifer was resigned and a little deflated, but with a full Saturday afternoon before her, she decided on a long run in Audubon Park to counter the encroaching bad mood. Even though it was a humid ninety-six degrees, excessive even by Memphis standards, it seemed like a good idea. She needed to sort through the bizarreness with Mark and the details of her trip. For her, running was the best way to put things in order.

For Mark Irvin, the police officer who delivered the tragic news on June 5 was only his first brush with investigators. Memphis homicide detectives were very curious about him, knowing he had called Jennifer the night she died. Detective Helldorfer said, "He was looked at right away, obviously." Irvin's fingerprints were part of the crime-scene investigation and he was asked, as Noura was, for a saliva swab for DNA testing.

Jackson, Tennessee, is slightly under ninety miles from Memphis. Mark Irvin's alibi was that he was home asleep. "If you're asleep. If you're home by yourself, alone, how can that be proven or disproved?" Sergeant W. D. Merritt queried.

In an interview with CBS correspondent Richard Schlesinger for *48 Hours Mystery,* Lieutenant Mark Miller, who was the initial case coordinator, said of Irvin "I think the common thought was 'Man, this guy likes to talk a lot.' He just kept coming back. He just kept calling. . . . You can look at this two ways. Either it's honest interest, concern . . . or he did it and he wants to know what we know."

Lt. Miller's involvement in the case was short lived. Not long after the investigation started, he was promoted and transferred. Ironically, the murder site was well known to him. Long before Jennifer purchased the house, Miller actually had lived for a number of years at 5001 New Haven.

The Memphis investigators arranged for Irvin to be interviewed by Jackson police. Those officers found no evidence implicating him in the murder. The defense questioned the thoroughness of these efforts. In his cross-examination of Lieutenant Miller, Art Quinn asked if Miller had requested that the Jackson police check Irvin's body for signs of a struggle. Miller said he "did not know." Pressed further by Quinn as to whether or not anybody corroborated Irvin's story or his whereabouts that night, Miller answered, "I assume not."

The image of Mark Irvin flashed before Ansley Larsson when she learned of Jennifer's death. "The truth is the first thing I thought of was [Mark]. There seems to be a seething—like a real underlying— anger with him that he appears to be a very controlling person."

Lieutenant Miller and Sergeant Merritt said they kept Mark "on the back burner and kept going forward with the case."

What was the purpose of Mark's phone call to Jennifer late that Saturday night? Was he too thinking of making the break final? Or did he feel bad that he had stonewalled the birthday visit she suggested? His intention went unsaid. Shortly before midnight he called Jennifer's cell phone from his cell phone and abruptly hung up without leaving a message. Too late to be calling he later testified. If Jennifer saw the missed call, she didn't return it. Had they spoken, Mark's would have been one of the last voices she heard.

In Absentia

"Perry said he went to Carter's house around dark before Italian Fest. He knew Carter was out of town and his house would be a good place to throw a party 'bash.'"—WMC-TV Trial Blog

"June 4, 2005. Everyone's at Carter's. There's beer, marijuana. They are at the house about three hours before Carter's grandmother, who lives down the street, came over and cleared out the party."
—WMC-TV Trial Blog

"It blew my mind. The freedom these kids had. They are coming and going all hours of the night. They all have cars. There is nobody checking on them. I mean they are totally free. They had too much money and too much freedom. They are looking for one party after another."—Detective Helldorfer

Noura and the girls moved from the bedroom toward the kitchen and the larger gathering. Noura's outburst about her mother registered hardly at all. Most everyone there mingled and enjoyed the summer night. Some, including Kaole, drank beer and smoked in the backyard. It was a repeat of Friday night except their host was absent. Carter offered the prefestival convenience of his house knowing he'd be out of town with his family and would miss the party.

That Saturday night at Carter Kobeck's house became a focal point in the prosecution's time line leading up to Jennifer Jackson's murder. Eleven of Noura's twelve friends were later asked if they had started the evening at Carter's. Only one, Andrew Hammack, had no connection to the prefest parties there.

On Tuesday, February 17, 2009, day eight of the trial, the prosecution included Carter on its witness list, along with six more of Noura's friends. Throughout the two-week trial, Carter and many witnesses first testified outside the presence of the jury—a 404 (b) hearing—and Judge Craft then ruled on what might and might not be mentioned when the jury reassembled in the courtroom. The defense, particularly Art Quinn in his cross-examinations of the young people, remarked often that it was amazing the witnesses could remember how much Noura was drinking or what kind of drugs she was using when their memories about themselves and their other friends were vague. Quinn began this line of questioning with Sophie Cooley and returned to that theme with others.

The string of young witnesses—one after another—prompted Clay Bailey, *The* [Memphis] *Commercial Appeal*'s blogger, to tag their series of testimonies "The Party Parade." After the trial, *48 Hours Mystery* reporters approached a number of Noura's friends, including Sophie Cooley, for interviews, though none of them were willing to appear on the program to talk openly about the matricide case.

For one juror, these young people were especially important witnesses. "I needed all of them," she said in an interview after the trial. "I wanted to hear them all. I could have heard more. They all said the same thing but in a different way. So you've *got* to be able to tell when someone is lying. I didn't think they were lying, but I enjoyed knowing that each one of them wasn't lying in their own crazy way. When you're dealing with teenagers and people like that, you need to get a story that's different that really makes a round circle.

And these kids, to me, I got the feeling that Noura supplied a lot of their drugs and that they kept Noura in the loop. I went to Talbots. The lady who works at Talbots—she helps me select my clothes—she used to work at Macy's. And she told me that right after Noura's mom died she came into [Macy's] and bought $900 worth of makeup brushes for all of those kids. So my instincts were right. These kids hung around Noura for what Noura could give and get from them."

The juror concentrated on making eye contact with the witnesses, the judge, and the lawyers. She looked at them to appraise their level of comfort with the situation and to determine if they are telling the truth. "You could feel the energy off them," she said. "The girls as witnesses were calm. They looked, but they didn't see. [Noura's girlfriends] came off as being superior to Noura, and they sat in the chair 'as if they owned the room.' They acted like the trial was not 'who they were. That they weren't really a part of it.'"

Had the context not been a murder trial, observers might have appreciated the attractive, youthful, and vivid personalities of the group even more. Detective Helldorfer said, "They were all great kids to talk with. They were very entertaining to interview. They were pretty open about everything that went on. From the drug usage to the sex. Even when it was showing a bad light on them. They were definitely scared. And they were worried about—repercussions from us? Nah. They were concerned about her getting out. Some of them were really scared of her."

Detective Helldorfer concluded the group had too much freedom and no discipline. "I don't know why the parents allowed it. I think the parents were young and trying to be their friends instead of their parent.

They are typical kids at this point. Thinking of drugs and sex. That's what's motivating them at this point. And I know the hormones are going strong. And that's where the parents need to come in and set guidelines. I don't think that was being done.

And Jennifer included. I'm not excluding her. Jennifer tried to be a friend instead of a parent, and I think that's the wrong approach."

Carter Kobeck, a handsome young man with dark hair and a mischievous smile, had troubles beyond involvement in Noura's murder trial. The evening before his testimony he was arrested for driving on a revoked license. He spent the night in the city jail located at 201 Poplar and appeared at Noura's trial in prison garb.

Colloquially the Memphis jail—a Dickensian muddle of humanity—is referred to as "201." Weekday mornings a public line forms that streams around the building. The line inches forward as all citizens must pass through security. From felons to individuals hoping to get a parking ticket dismissed; to distraught family and friends of victims or defendants; to mere trial observers, the morning crowd defies description. Worry, anguish, anger, impatience, crying children, and general despair infuse the swirl of people before they disperse to courtrooms. Then, about ten o'clock in the morning, it is as if a bomb dropped. The vast cavernous area clears, and as the day progresses, the building empties even more. It is possible over the lunch hour to ride down the elevator with vendors selling fried turkey legs.

Defense attorney Quinn asked why the witness was wearing jail clothes. "I'd like to know that, too," Carter quipped from the witness seat. (Detainees usually aren't allowed to stay in their civilian clothes.) Courtroom bailiffs reported Carter made a lot of outlandish requests while in the holding cell, like asking to order pizza and said he was excessively hyper about being in custody. Carter later refuted this in *The Commercial Appeal* blog. Coolly assessing Carter's behavior, Judge Craft said that if the bailiffs weren't going to get to him soon, they might have to get Carter a Lortab.

On his way to the witness stand from the lock-up area, Carter and Noura exchanged a friendly nod, one of the few times—besides with Alex and Perry—that Noura seemed affectionately connected with her old friends. She and Alex shared a conspiratorial smile as Alex talked about their plans to hook up Kaole with a girl at his house the Saturday afternoon before Jennifer's death. It was easy to imagine them laughing and plotting Kaole's romantic future. How things had changed. Alex was on her way to study in Italy; Noura faced the possibility of life in prison.

Throughout his lengthy questioning, Perry and Noura locked eyes as if there were no other people in the courtroom. "Brasfield stands to identify Noura," Clay Bailey blogged, "and the defendant even leans to her right so the witness has a clear look at her through the defense attorneys. She even smiles slightly when Brasfield describes what Noura is wearing as a black shirt and gray pants."

It all rattled Perry. He commented in the hallway after testifying: "I feel like the devil's child." But he also gave a friend the thumbs up sign.

Dressed in a jailhouse issued orange jump suit, Carter was asked during his 404 (b) hearing if he ever saw Noura act in a violent manner. He related two incidents. One a fight with a girl named Shannon near a friend's house in Cordova, an area near East Memphis. This scuffle occurred some time before Jennifer's death. (Noura visited the same friend, Eric Whitaker, at his house in Doe Trail Cove around 4:30 a.m. the morning of June 5, 2005, just before she said she found her mother's body.)

Carter's account of the altercation between Noura and Shannon included thrown punches and hair pulling. He said it was raining that night, and he sat in his car and watched the two girls fight in the street. Shannon fell and later wore a boot due to injuries suffered in the ruckus. He also said Noura slapped Perry that Saturday night, June 4, 2005, at his house even though he wasn't there. Later, Perry's testimony confirmed Carter's account. Judge Craft ruled the acts of violence would be excluded from Carter's trial testimony before the jury. Carter could only talk about his shared drug use with Noura. As it turned out, the prosecution did not call Carter Kobeck to testify before the jury.

Though an inconsequential witness as far as actual trial evidence was concerned, Carter set off a wave of intense and curious online comments in the Memphis daily newspaper's trial blog. Using first **thecarterk** and later his full name **carter kobeck**, he blogged, correcting fallacies as he saw them and chastising those unconnected on a personal level to the trial. One such avid contributor, **Paducahdry**, caught the wrath of Carter and his friends. **Paducahdry's** tirade infuriated the young people.

> **carter kobeck** Says: I love how i am portrayed as rich when my mother lives pay check to pay check and i have a job to pay for everything i need because i dont like taking my mothers money. Anyone who was in court saw pictures of my house . . . does it look like i live in some kind of mansion? you people are so ignorant it makes me sick. Where do you get my brain is fried? because i hadnt showered or slept

all night and didnt look my best? because my hair is messy because i was in jail overnight for a simple traffic violation? I'm sorry they didnt let me put on my clothes and dress appropriately i would have loved to but once again things werent done right and now lies are being told about me. . . .

carter kobeck Says: To you Paducahdry, who the hell do you think you are? some trial freak that wishes you were a lawyer? get a life you dont know me or anything about me. Im in college and am going somewhere in life besides my parents basement which is probably where you are. YES I SAID THAT I SMOKED MARIJUANA. O MY GOD CALL THE PRESS MARIJUANA. Man that just makes me totally brain dead loser druggie. You people are just too ignorant.

Some others chimed in with expressions similar to Carter's. They were angry that so many anonymous and uninvolved people were posting negative comments about the young witnesses.

NoName Says: . . . . carter dont worry about these ignorant morons we love you and know your not a trashball or a brain dead druggie. carter is really smart actually everyone he got screwed over . . . all of us involved with the trial or have friends that are including noura are going through a lot of crap right now. all

> of our nerves are shot. it is infuriating to get on here and see a comment posted bringing down someone that has testified b/c they were friends or family of noura. go get A LIFE!!!!!!

In his response to a post on a Facebook page created after the trial's outcome that was dedicated to Noura's innocence, Carter continued his online presence. Carter calls the writer an idiot who probably doesn't even know Noura.

> **Carter Jason Kobeck** your an idiot ive never even heard of you so you probably dont know her or what she was capable of . . . . she knew about it and had something to do with it the only question is who helped her? whose bloood was on the bed w her moms?
>
> March 19, 2009 at 10:04am

Social Media

***Sunnyd** Says: I so want to believe this girl didn't kill her Mom but I am beginning to have my doubts.*

***sissy** Says: This whole bunch of kids seemed to be irresponsible, undisciplined and unparented . . . They roved around like bands [of] gypsies night and day looking to [do] drugs and hook up. I think their testimony is irrelevant and doing nothing to prove the states case against Noura. It shouts 'we ain't got no evidence.'*

***NOURA=JAIL** Says: I went to school with Noura. She is guilty and anyone who really knew her would know that she, in fact, killed her mother.*

The media fascination—both traditional and social—with Noura's trial assumed a life of its own. Clay Bailey from *The Commercial Appeal* (which averaged 50,000 page views a day), and rotating reporters from local television station WMC, the NBC affiliate, blogged minute by minute from the courtroom. TruTv streamed video from the trial's outset that further fueled trial mania. Later, Noura's story was told on CBS's *48 Hours Mystery*. "My

Mother's Murder," the debut episode from Memphis, aired April 10, 2010, and again June 4, 2011.

Noura's trial was only the second time the Memphis daily newspaper assigned a reporter to the courtroom for a real-time blog. (The defense argued courtroom bloggers as a reason for acquittal or at least a new trial.) Blog followers posted opinions on everything from the "dry style" of the newspaper blog—"**John** Says: Clay Bailey's sparse description of trial events, live-blogged from the courtroom, at first blush is disappointing. Readers want COLOR. But, as the trial unfolds, his prose becomes elegant in its 'just the facts' simplicity. He also seems fastidious in his effort to present a case which could go either way. We're lucky as readers to have his dry style"—to the defendant, her family, various witnesses, lawyers, the evidence—or lack thereof—and legal strategies.

As the trial blog "community" evolved and identities were more apparent, name calling, feuds, and contentiousness broke out. The daily newspaper stories attracted their own following. Two online communities—real-time trial blog and newspaper story blog—confirmed a nearly insatiable interest in the fate of Noura Jackson.

Naturally, Noura's guilt or innocence was hotly debated throughout the trial and afterward.

> **Bob Dylan** Says: Um, no. She's guilty when the jury finds her guilty. Now, lets get [Andrew] Hammock in custody so we can all feel safe again.

> **GARRETT** Says: Once again Bob Dylan... Your obviously have nothing else to do besides

> going around posting comments. If [you] dont feel safe with Hammock not being in custudy, then gees you really have no life . . . obviously you dont though considering you posted as Bob Dylan.

Even Detective Helldorfer took note of the bloggers: "It blew my mind how so many people were taking sides who didn't know, who weren't in the courtroom. It was kind of surprising. That blogging stuff was new to me. I didn't know much about it before."

From the outset, *The Commercial Appeal (CA)* bloggers were remarkable in sheer number and radically diverse viewpoints. A few identified themselves as close friends of Jennifer and Noura, and attested to having intimate knowledge of the mother and daughter's private life (unconfirmed of course). Along with the merely curious, they all stoked the fire.

Emboldened by anonymity the posts were wild and varied—offensive, outrageous, colorful, and unintelligible. Entries ran the gamut. On day six of the trial **Marvin** appraised Jennifer's sisters—"At the risk of being sexist, all those Jackson sisters were some pretty fine skeezers, don't you think?"; and on day eight after Perry testified about bringing another girl to a party, he wrote, "Perry is lucky Noura didn't have her knives handy. She may have used him for a practice run."

> **NoRealProof** observed: I don't think there is any question Noura was on Drugs. As a short term neighbor, I saw a lot of activity that proved drug use and sales or a popular knitting class that made frequent 30 second stops.

Helldorfer said that by all accounts Jennifer was friendly and kind. People couldn't say enough good things about her. "Of course people tend to do that about a victim of crime," he added. Those manners failed in the online community where some felt no compunction *not* to speak ill of the dead. On day two of the trial **pbj** and **Lisa** depicted Jennifer as promiscuous. **Lisa** suggested Jennifer had a romantic relationship with Joe Cocke, the neighbor awakened by Noura that Sunday morning.

> **pbj** Says: Yea, Mom was busy running around in her sports bra and short[s] trying to look all hot in front of teenage boy. . . Outside on a major street corner . . . What can you expect a daughter to do??? Horrible mom . . . allowing parties . . . doing drugs herself . . . Apples don't fall far from the tree. Still no excuse for stabbing her mom but she was probably on drugs and didn't have control. . . . I have family on Newhaven and there were parties at that house all of the time. Teens drinking etc. . . . It was a distraction home for the entire street.

> **Lisa** Says: If Noura was a problem child at 14 what about the years prior? If you have a problem child as a single parent haveing men spend the night on a consistent basis does not help. She had a different man each month. Yes, Noura's behavior was out of control. But so was Jennifer's behavior. . . . MPD [Memphis Police Department] was very sloppy by not investigating the daughter's body nor the young man that went into the house with his gun. He had more than a business relationship with Jennifer.

Jennifer's advocates reacted strongly to this besmirching of her character.

> **whoa whoa whoa** Says: NONE of Ms. Jacksons actions justify murder. She was a sweet and caring woman. She was never trying to "look all hot" in front of teenage boys. She was an attractive, single woman, so she dressed fairly normally in my opinion. Also, it is not a uncommon sight to see a woman running in a sports bra and shorts in East Memphis. Noura was always a problem child. She often snuck out at nights to go drinking with her friends when she was as young as 14. Her behavior did not get any better as she got older, especially when drugs came into the picture. Ms. Jackson could not control her, but that does not make it OK for her to be killed.

On day eight of the trial, another blogger wrote about what she perceived as Noura and Jennifer's chaotic home life.

> **ICNOPROOF** Says: Let me say this . . . I lived near these two (Jennifer and Noura) and knew them very well. As much as I am so saddened by what happened to Jennifer, and she absolutely did not deserve this, her parenting to Noura was quite questionable. Her mother raised her in a home that was packed to the gills with crap everywhere (which was dysfunctional in itself), moved around A LOT, and her mother had a tendency to make bad choices (plus thrived on a lot of crisis)!!!! I can say that I witnessed a lot of "crisis" in their household. I always felt sorry for Noura when she was growing up because deep down inside she was a lost, lonely and sad little girl who couldn't figure out her life and was trying to fit in - and remember people, it's all about how you are raised. And I can say, her life was dysfunctional. I don't care if she did go to the most elite schools and live in rich neighborhoods, her life was MESSED UP!!! Obviously, she was an addict but much of her life and upbringing consisted of "crisis mode" and she apparently was filling a void.

A rare blogger—**f hall**—mentioned Noura's father:

> I knew Jennifer and Noura when Noura was a little girl. Jennifer was beautiful, inside and out. I knew Noura's evil father, also. That's how I got acquainted w/Jennifer. He told me he was going to get Noura and take her out of the country and Jennifer would never see her again. I found Jennifer and told her. He was an evil, despicable man who had a fixation on Jennifer, and anyone who remotely looked like her, as my daughter did. He is burning in hell and deserves to be. I hope Noura is innocent and if she is, I certainly hope it can be proven. She is a sad girl.

But an entry on the Facebook site supportive of Noura emphasized Noura's unhappy role in the middle of her mother and father's sturm und drang. It was a very different portrayal of Jennifer—"a furious woman" looking for Nazmi at his restaurant long after their divorce.

> **Frank King** Been away from Memphis for awhile now and was very surprised to see that her dad that I used to work for at Nora's Catfish House (he didn't spell it like her real name) in Southaven, MS was shot and killed in 2004 and then Noura being accused of murdering her mother. I remember when he used to bring her to work as a little girl and boy was she something else already. We may never know,

> but I think the relationship between her father and mother was affecting her more than we could imagine. I met Jennifer a few times when I managed his place and she would come looking for him. Pretty furious woman from my experience (bless her soul). I am not going to say the things Nazmi would say about her, but you can rest assure that they did not like each other and sorry to say but Noura was stuck in a tug of war between them. I didn't know her during her teenage years but I pray for her because if she continued to deal with the same issues in her teenage years as she did as a kid then I know she may have reached a melting point.

Amid the Internet clatter, fervid rumors, and actual testimony, startlingly different versions of Jennifer and Noura emerged. Posted comments and trial witnesses offered conflicting versions of the mother and daughter. Jennifer was a smart, beautiful, driven woman. She loved her difficult daughter and was committed to her well being. She was dedicated to friends and a spiritual person active at her church. A self-disciplined triathlete who enjoyed challenging herself. A devoted sister to her younger brother.

But other accounts introduced a status-conscious person seeking material wealth. An avid shopper who often bought in duplicate and more, and then left items unopened, never to be used. The items grew and grew until they overwhelmed and conquered her domestic space.

A series of unfortunate marriages—chronicled in divorce records—and an ill-suited relationship left her angry and "furious." One husband she couldn't count on for the child support payments; one husband cheated on her; and one boyfriend wanted more than she was prepared to offer.

Noura was manipulative, spoiled, narcissistic, threatening, and determined to get her own way. She was relentless in her efforts to get what she wanted. She indulged in alcohol and drugs. Sex was something she might offer to get what she wanted. If another girl got between Noura and her boyfriend, she would do whatever it took to regain his affection. School or work did not appeal to her. She was hedonistic and self indulgent. Things should be *for* and *about* Noura.

Noura struggled in school because Jennifer was an inconsistent, absent parent. At home there were few if any rules and no schedule. When she was young she was often tardy and missed school days. This could not have been the fault of a small child. This was Jennifer's failing. Instead of addressing problems, Jennifer would put her in a different school.

Noura was a lovely, affectionate, respectful girl who blended in with her friends' families and was always welcome. She was a sweet child who loved her mom and loved spending time with her. She loved animals and good times. She often was the life of the party, the center of attention. Her friends meant the world to her.

This unabashed personal scrutiny in an open forum would have horrified Jennifer, a woman described by her inner circle as modest and deeply private. These traits that were so central to Jennifer's character made the circumstances after the murder all the more monstrous. Murder victims not only lose their life but also their privacy. The family's victim impact statement, read at sentencing, emphasized this flagrant public intrusion; a direct result, they stressed, of Noura's selfish crime.

> Noura knows that Jennifer was extremely private and modest. It was the ultimate in contempt and humiliation to leave her exposed in death in the most intimate way for all the world to see—taking away her dignity and modesty, humiliating and de- humanizing her. None of this seems to bother Noura. Nor does it seem to make any difference to her that the death photos of her mother will be displayed to the public and splashed across television screens for the whole world to view as entertainment.

Matricide

Writing about psychic matricide and matricidal fantasies or impulses in The Undead Mother, *author Christina Wieland pursues Electra—"Alone at Argos with a murdered mother, in a blood-stained palace."[3] Despite her desire to kill her mother "out of hate and suffocation. The fact is that Electra cannot leave mother behind. Being a woman, Electra identified with her, and this identification with a damaged or murdered object is her fate."[4]*

Q. You did not regard her as your mother?
A. Not exactly, no; although she came there when I was very young.

Q. Were your relations toward her that of daughter and mother?
A. In some ways it was and in some it was not.

Q. In what ways was it?
A. I decline to answer.

---

[3] Christina Wieland, *The Undead Mother: Psychoanalytic Explorations of Masculinity, Femininity, and Matricide* (London: Rebus, Press, 2000), 119.

[4] Wieland, 42.

Q. Why?
A. Because I don't know how to answer it.

Q. In what ways was it not?
A. I did not call her mother.

Q. What name did she go by?
A. Mrs. Borden.—Inquest Testimony of Lizzie Borden, August 9, 1892[5]

Had Noura not attended five different Memphis schools creating a sizable network of "I know someone who knows someone who knows someone," her trial might not have been such a local sensation. What drew a broader and more diverse audience was the nature of the crime of itself.

Since the infamous Lizzie Borden case in 1892, the public has demonstrated a fascination with parricide (the killing of a close relative). Accused of killing her stepmother and father, Lizzie Borden's case became one of the first nationally prominent murder trials in the United States.

A thirty-one-year-old spinster, Lizzie lived at home with her elder sister, Emma; their notoriously ill-tempered and penurious father, Andrew Borden; and stepmother, Abby Borden, a shy woman without many acquaintances. Lizzie was not fond of Abby, whom she referred to as Mrs. Borden, rather than Mother, following a dispute between the two over a real estate transaction some five years before the murder.

---

[5] Linder, Doug. "The Trial of Lizzie Borden." 2004. *Famous Trials.* 2012. University of Missouri-Kansas City, UMKC School of Law. Web.

Lizzie discovered her seventy-year-old father's body at 11:10 a.m. on a sweltering August morning. He appeared to have been reclining on a sofa in the first-floor sitting room, though his feet rested on the floor. Sometime later sixty-four-year-old Mrs. Borden was found facedown on the floor of an upstairs guest room. Investigators determined Mrs. Borden died between 9:00 and 10:00 a.m., and Mr. Borden an hour or more later. Instead of the purported forty ax whacks from the children's rhyme, Abby Borden received eighteen to nineteen blows and Andrew Borden a mere eleven.

Significant trial rulings went Lizzie's way—her two inquest testimonies which revealed changing stories and the testimony of a drug store clerk that the day before the murders Lizzie tried to buy prussic acid, a deadly poison—were deemed inadmissible. The prosecution's case lacked a murder weapon or bloody clothing. Lizzie had burned a blue dress—the same color dress she wore the day of the murders—at the kitchen stove the day after her parents' funeral.

Compelling circumstantial evidence—including testimony that Andrew Borden planned to change his will in Abby's favor and theft of jewelry and cash from the master bedroom with suspicion falling on Lizzie—but in the end there was not enough for a conviction. One of the trials more chilling details came from Bridget Sullivan, an Irish immigrant in her twenties, and the Borden's live-in housekeeper. Bridget testified she heard Lizzie laugh from the upstairs landing as Bridget unlocked the front door for Mr. Borden. He had returned home about 10:40 a.m. Lizzie's mirthful exclamation would have occurred not long after Abby was killed upstairs.

There also was ample tension in the household. Some five years before the murder there was a brouhaha over a real estate transaction that excluded the Borden sisters. Their father had purchased a home and titled it to his wife and her sister, Sarah. In May of 1892, three months before his murder, Andrew and Lizzie argued over the pigeons Lizzie kept in the family's barn. Her father had killed them with a hatchet. Upon her death in 1927, Lizzie bequeathed the bulk of her substantial estate to the Fall River Animal Rescue League.

Soon after her acquittal, Lizzie and her sister Emma moved to a large home in a fashionable part of Fall River, Massachusetts, trying to separate themselves forever from the slights and vexations of Andrew and Abby Borden.[6]

A contemporary case with similarities to Noura's involved Donna and Ryan Young of New Port Richey, Florida. As in Jennifer and Noura's relationship, there was no evidence of abuse. To the contrary, Donna, like Jennifer, was a doting single mother of one.

Donna Young, fifty-two years old at the time of her death, appeared to capture the esteem and affection of those who knew her. Donna suffered from multiple sclerosis and was forced to use a metal walker or wheelchair. Her physician, Dr. Carlos Zubillaga, cautioned her against pregnancy and warned of potentially "dire consequences." But she wanted a baby and was thrilled at the birth of her son and only child, Ryan, in 1982.

[6] Ibid.

She was a single mother after her divorce from Ryan's father in 1994. A friend of eighteen years said "I think Donna wanted to make up for being a handicapped only parent. . . . I never heard the word 'no' too much from her. She never raised her voice."

Mike Halkitis, the assistant state attorney involved, said it was only the second matricide case in his thirty-one years of prosecuting criminals. In the other case, the son, after shooting his mother in the head, tossed her body in a pond "hoping alligators would dispose of the body."

"In that case," Halkitis said, "there was lots of friction. They fought. And the mother had a ton of money. Ryan Young is a different situation. There are mothers who abuse their children. This kid got everything. She paid his bills, gave him a car, sent him to a good school. What went wrong? You'd need a team of psychiatrists."

Ryan had a short-lived marriage in 2005 to a young girl his mother admired. Just months into the marriage he told his wife and mother he was gay. With the abrupt end of the marriage, Ryan, a clerk at a 7-Eleven store, continued to underachieve. His vehicle was repossessed, and his other debts soared. Donna bailed him out until one day she said no. It was at that point, prosecutors contended, that Ryan went to his mother's home one night and smothered her. He then staged an unconvincing burglary. Ryan, who was twenty-four years old when Donna died, and twenty-six years old at the time of his first-degree murder conviction, was sentenced to life in prison.

Over a practice spanning thirty years with thousands of patients, Dr. Zubillaga singled out Donna Young. "Nobody inspired me like Donna," he said. "When you have MS, you have an excuse, but I never heard any complaints from

Donna. She worked out and got extremely muscular, very strong and independent. That's just so unusual because MS patients get fatigued so easily. But she had great resolve, great focus."

"You could not feel sorry for Donna."

And, the doctor said, "She loved that baby."[7]

As evidenced by the attention parricide and matricide cases attract, they are uncommon occurrences. Kathleen Heide, Ph.D., and author of journal article "Matricide: A Critique of the Literature,"(*Trauma, Violence & Abuse*), told *Commercial Appeal* reporter Lawrence Buser that Noura's case was "very rare from age and gender.

Less than one percent of all homicides involves the killing of a mother by her offspring and less than 15 percent of those are girls 19 or younger."

Heide, a criminology professor at the University of South Florida, specializes in juvenile homicide. Generally, she noted, most children and adolescents kill to end abuse or get their own way. In "Q & A: Why Kids Kill Parents," posted on the *48 Hours Mystery* website, Heide profiled three categories of parricide offenders. Of the three types, Noura's profile most closely matched the dangerously antisocial child (DAC). Antisocial, as used in DAC, differs from the common sense of the word. Here antisocial is a reference to one's behavior toward others. Heide states

[7] Bill Stevens, "In Slaying of Pasco Mom, Son Faces Trial," *Tampa Bay Times*, 10 January 2009.

that DAC children have a "pattern of violating the rights of others when it suits them."

According to Heide, these DAC children or adolescents kill the parent to further their own goals. "In these cases, the parent is an obstacle in their path to getting what they want. These individuals, for example, may kill to have more freedom, to continue dating a person to whom the parents object, and to inherit money they believe eventually is coming to them." Heide cites the outset of DAC as beginning in childhood with a pattern of defiance, a strong personal agenda, and the refusal to accept responsibility for one's actions. Untreated, such children later frequently are diagnosed as having Oppositional Defiant Disorder (ODD). Symptoms of ODD include persistent tantrums, arguing, and angry or disruptive behavior toward parents and other authority figures. If that condition is uncorrected, it may elevate to Conduct Disorder and might include criminal activity, deceitfulness or theft, violence toward people or animals, destruction of property, and serious violations of parental rules such as "staying out all night or being truant from school."

Heide emphasized the importance of boundaries when raising children; of setting limits and enforcing discipline. "In parricide cases, I have seen good parents overindulge their children with fatal results. These parents often love their children very much and do not want to fight with them over 'little things.' The problem is that the little things become bigger and bigger issues. At 15, 16, or 17 years of age, the son or daughter in now saying 'I am going out. I am taking the car. I am dating who (sic) I want.'

"The parent appropriately steps in and says 'no.' However, youth has not learned that you do not always get your way. The youth has no frustration tolerance, meaning that he does not know how to deal with disappointment, and gets angry. Sometimes the anger is so intense that it erupts into a deadly rage."

The manner in which Jennifer's family portrayed Jennifer, the mother, and Noura, the daughter, in their victim impact statement was almost a textbook illustration of Heide's premise.

> Jennifer was the best possible mother, showering Noura with love, affection, attention, special birthday parties, creative holiday celebrations, Easter egg hunts and gifts beyond counting. Jennifer's life was centered around and entirely devoted to Noura. She did the best she could to understand and guide Noura and provide for Noura's best interest and future. Jennifer made great sacrifices for Noura and was repaid with anger, disrespect, betrayal, violence and a hideous, painful and bloody death.
>
> No amount of time will enable us to comprehend the brutal massacre of our beloved Jennifer by the daughter she loved most in the world. The horror of it all is only heightened by the fact that Noura has never shown any remorse, never shown any grief. It seems that she has no compassion, no sorrow, no regrets. She did not take so much as a moment to mourn her mother's death. Rather she was impatient to get back to an amoral life

> of drugs and partying. We are overwhelmed with sorrow for Jennifer, that she was made to suffer the ultimate betrayal and unimaginable death at the hands of her only child.

Two words repeatedly surfaced when characterizing Noura: spoiled and manipulative. For years her tantrums had been successful. "Yes," Helldorfer said, "She got what she wanted out of it. But her mother didn't do her any favors by doing it."

In an interview after Noura's trial, Helldorfer discussed an audiotape conversation between mother and daughter —taped by SunTrust Bank where Jennifer worked—that was "like someone flipped a switch."

"We heard her talking to Noura. Noura wanted a haircut, color, and a $150 pair of jeans. They'd been going along great, talking just fine. Noura was talking about how she was going to go to school and become a lawyer—which was a joke because she couldn't stay in school—and the conversation went to the haircut, color, and jeans. And when her mom said no, that's too much money, she turned on a dime like a banshee. And it was incredible to hear the turn. And her mother never raised her voice, tried to diffuse it, talked softly. That's the only actual voice I ever heard of [Jennifer's] but I was impressed by the way she tried to handle it."

Manipulative was an odd word, Helldorfer felt, for a group of eighteen year olds to use. Yet it was the word Noura's friends repeatedly chose to describe her. "They all said the same thing about her. They all used the same strange word—manipulative. Every one of them. And that's an unusual word for eighteen year olds. They all said she'd do whatever she wanted—whatever she had to do—to get what she wanted. Down to using sex to get what she wanted. If she was trying to get close to a guy, or a girl was with some other guy, she'd do whatever it took."

Are single parents more likely to create this codependent parenting pattern and less likely to assert control and discipline when necessary, thereby inadvertently fomenting a hostile relationship? Heide noted there is no national data that "record family composition of matricide victims," but based on her own cases and other professional clinical reports, she hypothesized that "female adolescents are more likely to kill mothers when they are in single family situations because of the added stress that their mothers may be experiencing. . . . These mothers often have the responsibility of supporting themselves and their children without significant financial and emotional support."

Firearms are the weapons of choice for juveniles and adolescents who kill their parents. Though Heide said, "About one in four juvenile matricide offenders stabbed their mothers to death. Adolescents who kill parents often act impulsively. Those who select knives are even more likely to act due to strong feelings rather than to conscientiously plan[ning] the killing. Knives are readily available in homes. Grabbing a knife and wielding it requires little planning."

Inflicting multiple wounds is even more primal than acting on the rage the juvenile is feeling. Multiple stabbing "is often the release of very strong negative emotion." A study involving rats showed that a positive feedback loop exists between aggression and the release of stress hormones—"stress and aggression form a rapid positive feedback loop. When stress increases, aggression increases. Conversely, aggressive behavior leads to the release of stress hormones."

Heide referenced several cases involving multiple stab injuries. "Once in this positive feedback loop, the offender continues to act out violently until his or her rage has dissipated. At this point, the offender is completely exhausted. Often offenders in this situation report later that they are stunned by what they did."

In her closing argument, Prosecutor Amy Weirich dramatically asserted that each stab wound Noura inflicted was retaliatory—*this* is for the money Noura wanted; *this* is for the freedom she wanted; *this* is for ostracizing Perry. "For every time Jennifer told her no," Weirich said, "that knife went in deeper and deeper."

When one juror echoed Weirich's assertion, saying—"And each stab was because of this . . . this stab was for Perry . . . this stab was for this . . . and I think she named off in her mind as rapidly as she could what each one of those was for"—it was clear the prosecution's argument had resonated with her.

However, biological research suggests that contrary to the notion that each stab wound was a conscious decision, the feedback loop indicates an inability to stop the attack. Thus when the offender initiates the assault, he or she loses the ability to stop, think, and conscientiously make choices. Those skills, according to Heide, are "severely compromised."

Noura and Jennifer's relationship appeared to mirror the classic characteristics of a troubled mother-daughter relationship. Although they were dependent on each other, they seemed to resent the dependency. Likewise, as Noura struggled through the normal separation process all girls encounter, her father was absent, compromising her ability to separate from Jennifer. A healthy father-daughter relationship can ease the transition.

Daughters, on one hand, naturally identify with their mothers as their femininity is evolving. At the same time, they are striving to be independent. It is a difficult and delicate balance under the best of circumstances.

Jennifer's damaged relationship with her own mother, Linda, might have contributed to her parenting difficulties. Jennifer and her sisters chose to live in Memphis as teenagers with their uncle and his wife, rather than with Linda. In an effort to advance his custody petition, Noura's father claimed in divorce papers that Jennifer's inability to mother was due to her own mother's maternal failings.

"Most psychoanalysts . . . agree that the main factor determining the quality of mothering, in any particular case, is the quality of mothering which the mother herself received as a baby, because mothering is a psychological and not a biological phenomenon."[8]

Noura's academic and behavioral problems surfaced before her teens. Her elementary school history showed a pattern of tardiness and absences. Her tendency to look for a mother figure in a number of her friends' mothers—Dana Fredrick; Ansley Larsson; Kathy Menkel, Anna Menkel's mother; Regina Hunt, who taught Noura Sunday

---

[8] Wieland, 107.

school; and later, her attorney Valerie Corder, took on more significance after Jennifer's death.

Ansley Larsson, like Dana Fredrick, found herself in the role of Noura's quasi-mother when Noura was dating her son in the eighth grade. After her arrest, several attorneys approached Noura offering assistance—one of whom is quite prominent locally for his successful defense of clients facing murder charges—but Noura chose Valerie Corder. Ansley believes Noura primarily made that decision based on Valerie's gender—"She picked Valerie because she's a mother." Noura told Ansley she felt Valerie would be more "hands on."

The dynamics and complexity of being a mother to a daughter as opposed to a son also present challenges. A study by British scholars Luise Eichenbaum and Susie Orbach cites evidence that mothers relate differently to their baby girls. They hold them less, breastfeed them less, and spend less time with them.[9]

The mother may see herself mirrored in her daughter, and that introduces difficulties. She may face an "unresolved conflict within herself (the split off, the needy little girl) [that] is projected onto the daughter."

Her relationship to her daughter may assume a highly inconsistent tone. "At times she will see her daughter as separate and—in that case—will be capable of being a good mother to her. At other times, however, she will see her daughter as part of herself, and will become either

[9] Wieland, 110.

rejecting or overly involved, or both—depending on how she herself relates to the part of herself which her daughter has become. . . . This inconsistency, this staccato quality, characterises the mother-daughter relationship."[10]

Some of Noura's friends and their mothers, as well as Nazmi's friend, Gloria, commented upon Jennifer's lax parenting style. For years Noura was essentially without a curfew and her activities unmonitored. Jennifer was hard working and career driven. She supported them both and was often at work or traveling for work. At home, she interacted with Noura more as her friend than her parent.

Noura was seventeen when Jennifer suddenly assumed the role of disciplinarian. Jennifer began saying no to Noura's demands. She insisted that Noura obey her: she would come home on time, do her school work, abstain from drugs, distance herself from Perry. Where had those rules been before now?

Jennifer's new role was most likely another form of inconsistency to her daughter. Noura apparently did not regard her mother as an authority figure, and she balked at any kind of restraint. While she waited for her mother's usual behavior to return, Noura grew impatient. They engaged in a tug of war with Noura becoming more rebellious and unmanageable as Jennifer became more persistent and vigilant.

Ansley Larsson and Dana Fredrick knew Jennifer as well as her daughter. Ansley's son, Max Quinlan, and

[10] Wieland, 111.

Noura were friends, even boyfriend and girlfriend in seventh through ninth grade years. "Jennifer Jackson's first priority was image," Ansley said. "How she looked to other people. And she wanted Noura to look and be perfect. She would shower us with gifts, and I was always uncomfortable with her generosity."

Dana Fredrick described Jennifer as "very elite, really nice, and kind of shallow," and Noura as "one of the most pleasant kids I've ever been around. She was very respectful of me, and I never heard her say a negative thing about her mother."

Ansley said Noura "loved, worshipped, and adored" her mother. At the time her son was involved with Noura, Ansley depicted Noura as devoted to her mother. Valerie Corder, Noura's lead defense attorney, told the jury of Noura's love for her mother. According to Valerie, while helping prepare her case and during the course of the trial, Noura stipulated nothing negative was to be said about Jennifer in her defense.

Ansley recalled that Jennifer could not stand to be home alone and called Noura to come be with her. She remembers Noura responding willingly, even canceling her own plans to be with her mom. Such a pattern of codependency and inability to separate frequently is cited in matricide cases, characterizing the relationship as mutually dependent and sometimes hostile.

This strange dynamic—*I want to be with you but I don't want to be with you. I want to be like you but I don't want to be like you*—creates tension and seems at odds with the strong, loving bond some mothers and daughters enjoy. Heide references such a bond in her work: "I believe it's stronger among daughters than sons. Little girls want to be like their moms and look toward [them] as their role models." Heide also notes that love doesn't seem to be lacking in most cases of matricide she has studied over the years. "At the end of the day, these girls really do love their mothers—that's the irony."[11]

"As sad as it is—and I'm sure in some way—Noura really loved her mother," one of the trial jurors said. "But if you've been around people that are addicted to drugs, you can love that person, but the drugs and that life style comes first."

Noura explained to Richard Schlesinger on *48 Hours Mystery* that she was spoiled by her mom but not spoiled rotten. "There was good rapport there," she said describing her relationship with her mother. "I felt comfortable with allowing my mom to know whatever was going on in my life. We didn't have any secrets and it was a two-way street."

Ansley interacted with Jennifer while their children were dating. On a few occasions, she stepped in to insist on more supervision for her son and Noura. Jennifer was impressed, almost surprised, by that level of parental involvement. She began calling Ansley for "good mother advice."

When Ansley caught Max smoking marijuana the summer before his tenth grade year, she grounded him for a month. And she enforced it. "Noura would come over," she said, "but I think she just got tired of waiting for him." They broke up that summer though Noura continued to stay in

[11] "Q&A: Why Kids Kill Parents." *48 Hours*. CBS News, 26 July 2012. Web.

touch with Ansley. She called her one time, crying, asking if Ansley would pick her up because her mother wouldn't.

Ansley characterized Jennifer as an inconsistent, often absent mother. "Jennifer had no sense, no clue, how to be a mother. She was famous for not following through," Ansley said. "She was the worst mother I ever saw. She treated Noura as if she was an annoying younger sister." Noura's eighteenth birthday celebration involved a limousine ride to Florida with friends. Jennifer drove the limo and she even wore limousine driver's livery. Ansley wondered why Jennifer just couldn't be a "normal" mother. "But she couldn't."

Yet, from Nazmi's friend Gloria's perspective, Jennifer and Noura's relationship wasn't "different from any other mother and daughter when the daughter reaches Noura's age. Noura was seeking more independence," she said. If anything, Gloria found Noura to be "more passive than aggressive. She was smart and mature for her age." Gloria said she believed Noura's problems started with the death of her father.

When Sophie Cooley spoke of Jennifer's restraint with Noura in terms of money, she was the exception. "Her mom was very financially responsible," Sophie said. "And her mom would tell her things like 'I'm not going to pay for you to get your hair done at Capelli and spend $150. Your friends can do that but you're not going to do that.'" Ansley, however, regarded Jennifer as too indulgent: "Jennifer gave her anything and everything she wanted and let her do anything and everything she wanted." Paradoxically, Ansley felt this lowered Noura's self-esteem, as she never had to develop and discover talents she might possess. "Noura was spoiled rotten and a little self centered," Ansley said. "But if you were ever given a chance to spend time with her, you'd love her."

Ironically, Ansley said Noura "flourished" while she was in jail, though now that Noura is in prison, Ansley said she "suspects it is much harder for her."

"[Noura] blossomed as a person. She discovered she cared about other people, and that she had skills that would be valuable."

Judge Craft concurred with Ansley's observation about Noura's damaged self-esteem. Craft saw Noura's entire group as searching for more positive self-image; a group willing to use drugs to feel better about themselves.

"Their parents" he said in an interview, "were more concerned with their own lives than with their children's. Wealthy children at private schools are like very poor children except they have resources; they live off of trust funds. Poor kids don't have Lortab and prescription drugs; they have crack. Both groups lack self-esteem and turn to drugs to get numb, to forget their lack of self-esteem. These wealthy kids develop self-esteem issues because they aren't accomplishing anything on their own. Their esteem becomes tied to what they are given, material possessions. They are seeking the wrong things."

The culture of modern-day, excessive parental indulgence was a recurring theme in the trial. Noura's own witness statement is a fascinating reflection of her absorption with material goods. Noura was fuzzy on many details, and though eighteen years old at the time, she did not know her social security number and was not employed.

But when asked about Richard Raines' vehicle—her ride Saturday night from Perry Brasfield's back to her car at Carter Kobeck's—she was uncharacteristically precise in her response: "A 2005 Z71 black Tahoe." Her mom had a "really nice cell phone . . . a high tech cell phone . . . Burberry or something like that." She herself drove "a Jeep Cherokee, silver."

Through Perry's Window

"Prosecutor Steve Jones asked Perry if Noura slapped him. He said yes because he was with another female at Carter Kobeck's. [Judge] Craft said that is what he expected was the reason. That even causes Noura to smile."—Commercial Appeal *Trial Blog*

A frenetic energy swept over the group at Carter's house. Should they go to the Italian Fest? Or not? Free radicals bouncing off of each other. Noura found it fatiguing. "My mom's a bitch and she needs to go to hell." The words rang again in her head. So awful. So hateful. Tonight her anger made her feel odd, as if her head wasn't in the same place as her body.

And then the second bombshell. Perry showed up at Carter's with another girl! Noura couldn't believe it. She thought they were on their way to being a couple again. Before Florida he told her "it wasn't working out [for them]." But since she'd come back, they had been talking a lot, and she assumed they would be together tonight. Noura even told Andrew that Perry was back in the picture; that she and Andrew would just be friends.

All the possible reasons Perry was with someone else swirled like an eddy current in her mind. She blamed her mom. It sucked that she was so unreasonable about Perry. She knew it bothered him to have fallen into Jennifer's disfavor. She'd demanded the house key back from him (the one he had for house sitting) and continued to threaten him with a restraining order. Restraining order?! How many nights had Perry eaten dinner with them, watched movies, and hung out?

Perry probably wouldn't be described as a heartthrob—dark, almost reddish hair, average height, and a stocky build. But he was for Noura. When Noura first met him, and before he was expelled for fighting, Perry was a student at Christian Brothers High School. The altercation that ended his studies there occurred in a Cordova movie theatre following a football game between Christian Brothers and Memphis University School. While the schools enjoy a healthy rivalry, fighting is not tolerated.

Perry lived across the street from Dana Fredrick and her daughters, Lindsey and Natalie, two of Noura's best friends. And at the time Noura met Perry, Noura practically lived there too. "She was a delightful young lady," Dana said in an interview. "She basically had her own room and was inseparable from my daughters for two years. Had there been a darker side to Noura, I would have picked up on it. Something would have raised a red flag to me and there were no red flags, ever."

Then, in September 2004, Dana's eldest daughter, Lindsey, left for the University of Tennessee; Natalie moved to Midtown Memphis; Dana sold her house and moved to Cordova; and "Noura went home."

Dana felt Noura was seeking more stability in her life: "There was more a sense of a family unit at our house, and Noura thrived. A happy, outgoing, delightful child in my home. It never occurred to me to say, 'maybe Noura should go home.'"

With the Fredrick family's diminished role in her life, Noura spent more time with Perry and a new group of friends. When Natalie saw her some time later, she found Noura withdrawn and felt she had taken a bad turn. "She'd gone downhill, emotionally especially," Natalie said.

Noura and Perry saw each other almost daily from late 2004 to June 2005. They were together constantly except for short breakups, going to movies, spending time with friends, and at each other's houses.

The girl with Perry at Carter's Saturday night was Britney, his "new lady friend," as he described her during his trial testimony. She went to Germantown High School with him. Noura was crushed and humiliated in front of their friends. For a while she avoided them but couldn't help but notice when Perry kissed Britney. Noura felt cast aside. How easily he had moved on without her! She walked briskly toward Perry and the interloper, as Noura regarded her. In no time she and Perry were in a heated discussion. That rage she'd felt earlier when talking about her mom surged again. She shocked herself when she slapped Perry. That sent Britney fleeing for the rest of the evening; and shortly thereafter, Carter's grandmother appeared and hustled everyone off the Kobeck property.

Evicted from Carter's house, Noura's group made its way to Italian Fest. Kaole remembers bumping into Noura once while there and then walking with her from Marquette Park back to Carter's house. Kaole's plans took him elsewhere, but Noura and the others formed a car caravan. They'd heard about a party in Midtown Memphis on Belvedere.

The oppressive and inescapable humidity that had been building all day now clung like a water-soaked blanket. Italian Fest had not improved Noura's mood. The first night is always better than the second, she thought. The Lortabs she'd taken, the weed, and the beer made her feel dull and had done nothing to ease her cramps. She was miserable.

Pretty much everyone wanted to check out the Midtown party. Noura felt bloated and a little leery of the white skirt now that she calculated the onset of her period. Perfect! She decided to change out of the skirt and gold sandals. She knew a way into Carter's house and grabbed a bag of clothes from her vehicle and went inside to change. She looked through her bag and settled on something safer, a dark-wash denim skirt and Teva flip-flops. Grabbed a jacket too.

When she walked outside people were jockeying around for places in cars. She'd already decided she didn't want to drive, but what she did want was to get in Perry's car. She realized she was tired of hanging out with all these people. She wanted to be alone with him. Even with Britney gone it seemed he still was keeping his distance.

Too late, they were all loaded into cars. Soon they left Carter's in a more organized fashion that most would imagine after two parties come and gone. But along the way she talked them into pulling over in the parking lot of Holy Communion on Walnut Grove Road. It was her church, and she knew in the morning her mom would be after her to go to Sunday school. Something else to dread! Once the cars stopped she jumped out and got in with Perry.

The Belvedere party was a nonevent so the "party parade" migrated to Perry's house in Germantown. They sat around the pool and talked. Several commented on how quiet Noura was and how often she repeated that she had to go home. That was news because Noura's curfews had never been heeded before. While at Perry's, Kirby and Sophie noticed Noura's different attire.

"When we went to Perry's house in Germantown later, she came over in a Patagonia, which was weird," Sophie said in an interview with journalist Lauren Lee. "She looked dead. I mean she was just blank the whole time we were there. But I mean she had been taking pills the whole time, so I don't think anyone noticed it. That's when we were talking about our parents and having to be home, because it was like really late. But . . . she's always been the loud one. She has to be the center of attention. So for her to just sit there, that's weird."[12]

Noura made no progress with Perry. He was distracted, and she later learned he was planning to meet Sophie at her mom's house on Williamsburg Lane in East Memphis. (The same street where Jennifer had attended a wedding reception earlier in the evening— the Fuller house at 375 Williamsburg Lane; the Cooley house at 525 Williamsburg Lane.) Sophie's mom was out of town and Brooke was spending the night. They had no curfew worries and looked forward to extending the party when Perry and Joey McGoff came over. First though, there had to be a smooth transition with Noura.

The party at Perry's broke up around midnight. When Noura's cell phone rang at 12:10—her mom!—she walked away from the others seeking some privacy. She figured Jennifer would be mad, and she was right. She was furious Noura had defied her again. She railed that Noura knew she was grounded. Her school work was unfinished as were her few chores. Noura listened as her mom promised more crackdowns and repercussions. Jennifer finally told Noura she was going to bed, but she expected her home now! They were going to church in the morning. Noura told detectives

---

[12] Lauren Lee "Jackson's Former Friend Talks About the Case." *Media and the Courtroom: The Noura Jackson Case.* 7 April 2011. Web.

the next day that was the last conversation she had with her mom.

Curfews started popping up for the others too. Clark's was at 11:30 and his mom picked him up. Kirby already had left to meet her midnight curfew. That left Sophie, Brooke, and Noura to find another way home. They wound up catching a ride with Richard Raines. Richard was one of the few party participants who did not testify at Noura's trial. According to Ansley Larsson, the prosecution wanted Richard to testify that Noura was acting odd that night. He wouldn't do so because he didn't think she *was* acting odd.

Sophie acknowledged the idea to ditch Noura was hatched at Perry's house. Brooke added, "It wasn't a big plan throughout the entire night—like everyone thinks—to go back to Sophie's." Whatever the specifics, Noura intentionally was excluded. Clearly Perry was more interested in Sophie at that point, but Joey also joined the cabal, even though he and Noura were close friends. They saw each other a couple of times a week; he'd had dinner at her home with her mom and uncle. (He also spent significant time with Noura after Jennifer's death, enjoying the liberties of no parents around.)

Perry's house cleared out except for Joey who was spending the night. Richard first took Noura to her vehicle back at Carter's and then dropped Sophie and Brooke at Sophie's where Perry and Joey joined them about an hour later. They stayed until 5 a.m.

It seemed Noura really was in the dark about Perry's plans with Sophie. After leaving his house at midnight, Noura persisted, calling his cell phone, pleading to talk about getting back together. She told Perry that she was on her cell outside her house smoking. Perry recalled being "very short with her" when he did answer her call. He already had plans. A text message at 1:13 a.m. was Noura again saying she wanted to be together. Wanted to talk about things. That text went unanswered.

Despite Noura's best efforts that Saturday night, Perry was resolute and avoided her overtures to reconcile. But within a few weeks of her mother's murder, Noura showed up at Perry's house. One summer night Perry heard Noura calling to him. He looked down and she was standing outside his window. There was a ladder nearby which he told her to use to climb up to his bedroom. Soon all was forgiven; they made up and had sex. "We made up for lost time, you know?" Perry said.

After that, Noura and Perry were once more attached. They spent their time using a plethora of drugs, rekindling their sexual relationship, and avoiding any discussion of Jennifer's death.

Rolling on XTC

He wishes now he had talked with Noura, maybe gone over there at 1:00 a.m., "It probably hadn't happened yet and maybe I could have helped clear her mind from doing it."—Interview with Andrew Hammack

Andrew may have missed the pre-and-post Italian Fest parties, but he and Noura were texting and talking throughout the night of June 4 and morning of June 5. Andrew thought it a little peculiar, as they hadn't been in touch in the days preceding Jennifer's death. They were an off-and-on couple, as Perry cycled in and out of Noura's life. Before her trip to Florida, Noura and Andrew weren't talking much since Perry was back in the picture.

Prior to that they had been seeing each in a steady fashion, several times a week. In fact, Andrew had been at Noura's house three weeks or so before Jennifer's death—in Noura's room, the living room, kitchen, sunroom, and by the pool in the backyard where he was playing with the dog. It wasn't an angry breakup, and they agreed to just be friends.

Andrew felt Noura's spate of phone calls to him on June 4 and the early morning hours of June 5 were "weird," given their circumstances. "She wanted to meet up, or whatever, at her house," he said in an interview. He didn't go in part because they hadn't seen each other in a week.

Investigators found Noura's interactions with Andrew strange as well. Like Mark Irvin, Andrew was asked for a DNA sample, and his fingerprints were analyzed. Eventually, police procured three separate witness statements from him. Detective Helldorfer said in an interview, "We didn't discount somebody helping Noura. But I think in everybody's mind when the cell phone records came in we could analyze—she's on the phone—da-da-da—nonstop. She stops, the killing takes place, then they start up again. She's looking for an alibi. We're pretty convinced there's nobody else but her."

On Saturday, June 4, Andrew said in his first statement, he talked with Kaole and Noura. "I talked to Kaole and [Kaole and Noura] were just riding around and hanging out. It was between 4:00 and 6:00 p.m. . . . Later on between 11:00 p.m. and 1:00 a.m. [June 5], I called her and she said she was on the way home from a party, she was by herself and she told me to meet her at her house in 15 minutes. I called her 15 minutes later when I got back to my house and she told me that she was in front of her house waiting on me. I told her that I was at my house and then she said she was about to go inside and she would talk to me later."

At 3:50 he again initiated contact with Noura. "I texted Noura at 3:50 a.m. and asked her what she was doing. She texted me back at like 4:28 a.m. and said she was sitting at Eric's and she wanted to see me. At 4:30 (I texted her) I told her that I wanted to see her too. (I was on my way back from Krystal and Ian was with me . . . I was going to drop Ian off and go to her house, but when I got to my house, I just went to sleep and I had been drinking and I didn't want to drive.) Then, at 5:00 she texted me telling me to "answer", but I didn't get it until the next morning [June 5]. I called her back at 10:59 a.m. and she didn't answer, but I already knew her Mom had been killed when we passed by the house that morning. I had tried to call her and get in touch with somebody, but I couldn't, so we drove past the house it was like around 11:15 a.m."

Noura also called Andrew on her way back from Eric Whitaker's house in those early morning hours. "She said she was on the way back from Eric's and she wanted me to come and meet her at her house and walk in with her. She said, 'Just come over. Just come in.'" While Andrew thought her request was bizarre, the prosecution considered it sinister.

Noura's call was followed by a succession of calls or text messages in the minutes before and after 5:00 a.m.: 4:47 a.m., 5:00 a.m., 5:01, 5:02, 5:03, 5:06. In his second statement to MPD, Andrew confirmed that he also received a call from the Jackson residence land line that he did not answer. Andrew was not the only one to get a call from the Jackson home. Clark Schifani was among the first to leave Perry's house Saturday night. When his mom picked him up around midnight, most everyone else was still there. He came home, and went to bed, and woke up the next morning to a call from a Memphis police officer who asked him to check his cell phone. Clark had two missed calls he'd slept through. He told the officer his cell phone address book showed a missed call from "Noura's home," at 12:59 a.m. and a call from "Noura's cell" at 1:09 a.m. with a voice message. Clark testified that he "knew Jennifer well," but she had never called him before. The prosecution saw the quick hang-up call to Clark as another linchpin—Noura was home after all.

Lieutenant Mark Miller testified that the last home line call was made from one of the two cordless phones on Noura's bedside table. That call was to Andrew's cell. Noura's cell phone history revealed her last call was to Andrew's phone. When Andrew woke up Sunday morning, June 5, he read a text from Noura sent at 5:00 a.m., "Answer." And a voice message, "I need to talk to you."

Andrew regarded Noura's suggestion that he "just come in" outlandish. He insisted that was something he had never done and would not have done.

"IF I were going over there at 1:00 a.m. it would have been to sit in my truck, in front of her house, not go inside," he said. "For her to suggest I just 'walk inside,' was 'beyond extremely unusual,'" he said.

Andrew met Noura five or six months before the murder. He said they met through friends while he was in school in Olive Branch, Mississippi, a Memphis suburb. He wasn't a frequent guest at the Jackson home like many of Noura's friends. He hadn't had dinner with Noura and her mom, and if he was in their home, Jennifer was away.

Andrew perceived Jennifer as tough on Noura: "Her mom was pretty strict on her. She would get mad when Noura spent money on junk, things that weren't necessities." Yet he said Noura never was without funds. "She always had money. Not a lot, but sometimes a few hundred dollars."

He added that "Noura complained about her mom more than most people her age." He felt Noura was discontent. She noticed what other people had; commented on what their lives were like "that she envied." But during that time, he never saw anything that alerted him to a possibly violent side of her personality. Certainly nothing that would make him "talk to the police or even Noura's mom."

He wishes now he had talked with Noura, maybe gone over there at 1:00 a.m., "It probably hadn't happened yet and maybe I could have helped clear her mind from doing it."

Looking back, Andrew believes Noura was trying to set him up—make him a scapegoat—with all of the phone calls and texts. When he heard of Jennifer's death he said that while he "for sure didn't see it coming," he somehow wasn't "shocked."

"At first I felt she did it," he said. "And I probably lost some friends over saying that—and then I felt *maybe* she didn't do it." The voice messages she left him that that night "did not sound extremely upset. And that made him think she did do it."

"I still don't know," he repeated more than once. "There's so much I still don't understand. The only people who will ever know are Noura and her mother."

Andrew as Noura's co-conspirator was a theory not that far-fetched for some on the jury. At the outset of deliberations two jurors believed Andrew took part in the actual attack. But eventually, the jury discarded that hypothesis, settling instead on the notion that he was primarily Noura's cocaine connection and someone she tried to set up. According to one juror, they found his testimony as "a friend with benefits" unusual and quirky.

"He looked at the floor and at Noura. They were quick looks like 'I can't believe you did that.' His eyes darted quickly over to her and seemed to express 'You really tried to drag my ass into this.' The look was not one of anger but 'a knowing look,'" a juror said.

Andrew said he was nervous about testifying in a murder trial, and he didn't want to make Noura look bad because they had been friends. When Andrew testified that on Saturday night "I had been drinking and couldn't afford a DUI at the time. I still can't," he drew a laugh from the courtroom as well as the jury.

For detectives, Andrew's various accounts of the night and morning in question were scattered. As they pushed for clarity, the interrogations, to Andrew, became "harsh and strange." He provided witness statements on June 7, June

10, and June 17, 2005. He said he felt like a suspect and that "they were trying to get stuff out of me."

Andrew testified at trial that at 12:30 a.m. on June 5 he gave a friend a ride home to meet his curfew. The friend, Bucky Shultz, lived in East Memphis, within a mile of the Jackson residence. He said he stayed at Bucky's house at least two hours. (Yet in his third statement Andrew said that Bucky didn't come out that night because he had the ACT in the morning, although it would be unusual to take the ACT, a standardized test, on a Sunday morning.) After leaving Bucky's, Andrew said he picked up his friend Ian and headed to a strip club. They first stopped for gas, drove around smoking marijuana, went to a fast food hamburger place, Krystal, and eventually made their way back to Andrew's house without ever making it to the strip club.

Defense attorney Quinn vigorously questioned Andrew about the two unaccounted for hours. Could anyone substantiate his alibi for the 1:00 a.m. to 3:00 a.m. time period? Did anyone talk with Bucky Shultz? It later was confirmed no one had spoken with or attempted to talk with Bucky Shultz.

Andrew's roommates also were suspicious of the time gap. So much so they took shoes Andrew had worn that weekend to the police. Since the group apparently used drugs shortly before their meeting with police, detectives found it nearly impossible to sort out their tale of the New Balance shoes. Lieutenant Miller described the group who brought the shoes by as "almost incoherent. They just showed up with the shoes," he said. At one point during the group's visit to Memphis Police Department's Homicide Division, detectives Mirandized Andrew's friend Eddie Zahed.

Miller gave the shoes to Detective Connie Justice who had taken Noura's witness statement on June 5. Justice photographed the New Balance tennis shoes, but no further testing was performed and the shoes were returned. To further muddy the waters, Noura was wearing a pair of gray New Balance shoes newly purchased by her mom during their trip the weekend before. Jennifer's blood was on the left and right laces of Noura's shoes and the left sole.

Andrew said his roommates were confused. They believed he was wearing a pair of New Balance tennis shoes on the night of June 4 that were "too small for him," and took those shoes to the police. The shoe visit remains quizzical. Andrew testified that the shoes in question belonged to his buddy, Garrett. Andrew said on the morning of June 7 when he gave his first statement, he slipped Garrett's shoes on, and, since they fit, he wore them downtown. He said he actually was wearing flip-flops the weekend of June 4 and June 5. And that his friends were "messed up on drugs when they took [the shoes] to homicide."

What his friends thought was significant enough about the sneakers to visit homicide is anyone's guess. The relevance of the New Balance shoes was never revealed during the trial or otherwise.

Andrew's second witness statement was elicited based on information from one of Jennifer's sisters. She had overheard conversations about Andrew wanting to tell the police something, but "he was scared." In this statement he told police about the land line call from the Jackson residence. The time period for the call, he said, was between midnight and 5:00 a.m. He also told them Noura wanted him "to meet her outside and walk inside with her."

Neither official statements nor Andrew's actual court testimony offered a consistent narrative of the missing two hours. In his first statement, he recalled taking Bucky Shultz home to meet his 12:30 a.m. curfew and said he stayed at Bucky's house for two hours. In his third statement, Andrew wrote that he partied with Ryan Greisham and others from midnight until almost 4:00 a.m. However, Ryan Greisham told the defense team's private investigator, Clark Chapman, that he was in Oxford, Mississippi, the weekend of June 4 and 5 for a college visit at the University of Mississippi.

Since Noura's defense team did not see Andrew's handwritten third statement until five days *after* the verdict came in, they argued in one of twelve issues before the Tennessee Court of Criminal Appeals that the State suppressed the statement. Further, they said, the statement was material and entitled Noura to a new trial. Judge Alan E. Glenn delivered the lead opinion of the Court of Appeals in which it affirmed the judgment of the trial court presided over by Judge Craft.

"According to the defendant," Glenn writes in the eighty-two page opinion, "[Andrew's third statement] reveals that 'on June 4-5, 2005, Hammack was intoxicated on street Ecstacy, a hallucinogenic, amnesiatic substance, and also was using marijuana,' that inconsistent with his previous statements, he admitted he was at a movie theater 'within yards of the decedent's home after 1 a.m.' on June 5, and that he was driving around until 3:37 a.m. when he went to a 'bar featuring nude entertainment,' all facts not disclosed in his first two statements. The defendant argues that these statements contradict Hammack's prior statements and trial testimony and 'establish that [he] either repeatedly lied to the police about his conflicting alibis, activities, whereabouts, and substance abuse' during the time the crime occurred or show that 'he had drug induced ante-grade amnesia, frontal lobe disturbance, confusion, and confabulation as to his conduct on June 5th.' Had the third statement of Hammack been timely provided, the defendant argues, he would have been cross-examined about the differences between it and his first two statements, including his whereabouts between 1:00 a.m. and 3:37 a.m. on June 5."

Judge Glenn concluded that "While it is true, as pointed out by the defendant, that Hammack's third statement differed somewhat from his first two statements, we cannot conclude the addition that he was 'rolling on XTC' or had been in the vicinity of the victim's house that evening, had it been disclosed, would have changed the verdict."

Noura's defense no doubt disagreed with Judge Glenn's findings, yet all involved probably would concur with his summation of Andrew's statements to police. "Hammack's statements," Glenn writes, "are rambling, somewhat difficult to follow, and became more confusing when an attempt is made to try and compare them."

His third statement, handwritten on University of Memphis correspondence addressed to his roommate Eddie Zahed, chronicles his activities on June 4 and 5, and best illustrates the chaos of Andrew's memory:

On Saturday June 5th close to midnight me, Ian, Jayron, and Marcus went to pick up [B]ucky from his house and he didn't come out because he said he had the ACT in the morning. So we met up with R. G. [Ryan Greisham] at the [P]aridiso [an East Memphis movie theatre] after we left Bucky's. I then got in the car with Ryan and we went to Matt Milner[']s and then we went to a party with Ryan. We were at the party and Noura called Ryan's phone looking 4 me because I left my phone with Ian and he told Noura I was with Ryan. We were at this party for a lil bit the[n] we left because Ryan tried to start a fight. Then we went back and met Ian, Marcus, and Jayron which they were in my truck. I got in my truck [I]an was driving Marcus in front Jayron in the back asleep. So then Ian drove us back to the house. When we got back to the house we came inside ([I] wanted to come home because I was rolling on XTC so we came home.) [L]ater on [Ryan] Greisham called and asked if he could come over. We sat here (house) for a while then Andrea and Chelsea came over. By this time [E]ddie was asleep because [E]ddie's g/f doesn't like Chelsea being at our house. At 3:57 me and Ian wanted to go to the strip club. We were on [G]etwell and we stopped at a gas station and me and [I]an decided to go back home. When we got there [A]ndrea and [C]helsea had left, when I got there [I asked] if Whit and [G]arrett

[were] still up. About 10 min[utes] later Ryan called Matt Milner and he wanted to hang out so me, Ryan, and Garrett went to Matt['] s and he didn't open the door so we left and came back home. We fell asleep then [E]ddie came downstairs in the morning and woke me, [I]an, and [J]ayron up and [E]ddie told us Noura's mom got killed last night.

Eighteenth Birthday

"It's my money! Give me the money! I want my money!"
—Noura Jackson to Jennifer Jackson

"Happy Eighteenth Birthday! I love you so much. I hope your eighteenth birthday is a special as you are!"—Jennifer's birthday card to her daughter

When Noura walked out of Ridgeway High School on March 17, 2005—her birthday and St. Patrick's Day—she was surprised to see one of her father's limousines parked in front of the school. Standing beside the car was her mother decked out in chauffeur's livery, complete with the silly hat! Jennifer was all smiles, and Noura could tell she was delighted with herself for pulling off this elaborate caper. Noura noticed how nice it was to see her mother smile. They had been so fiercely locked in battle over her dad's estate that they were both exhausted.

Attention usually was something Noura craved, but at that moment she didn't know if she should feel honored or mortified. Soon a couple of her friends joined her and let her in on the surprise birthday trip. They were all going to

Destin, Florida, a resort town on the Florida panhandle, and Jennifer was driving the limo. This trip to Destin, Noura imagined, was a truce of sorts. That morning her mother had given her a sweet birthday card.

While it may have been a good idea for the actual ride to Florida, driving a stretch limo around the crowded Destin roads was a little tricky. One night when they were out for dinner, Jennifer bumped another car. She'd had a few beers, and the driver insisted she cover the damage to his vehicle. Since clear titles to Nazmi's fleet of cars had eluded her, Jennifer had little choice but to pay for the incident out of her own pocket. She thought the other driver was rude and pushy. But she was relieved when he agreed not to report the accident. Jennifer realized she should have known better than to use one of Nazmi's vehicles. Now there was a hex on the trip. His damn cars were a bane.

The unrest Nazmi brought into Jennifer's life came early and stayed late—as late as his memorial service in January 2004. She and Noura exchanged angry words at the visitation. What about is still unclear. His death ratcheted up the tension between them. Noura, sixteen years old at the time, suddenly was thrust into the center of a very adult situation as she made decisions regarding her father's burial. When she tried to offer advice, Jennifer was rebuked. Eventually Noura wrote a check from Nazmi's account to cover the costs of returning his body to Lebanon.

Nazmi's friend, Gloria, like Jennifer and Noura, had viewed the security tape of Nazmi's shooting at the Memphis Homicide Division. And for some reason Gloria was the person the mortuary called: "They kept calling me and saying 'The body is ready,'" she said in an interview. Gloria had neither Jennifer nor Noura's phone number. Finally, Nazmi's brother, Awad Hassanieh, arrived from Lebanon and helped take charge of the arrangements.

Gloria spent a good bit of time with Awad. She learned that Noura was the family's first grandchild, even though Nazmi was the baby of the family. Awad described how his mother, Hodo Hassanieh, whose first name originally had been Noura's middle name, especially doted on Nazmi.

While cleaning out Nazmi's apartment, Gloria and Awad discovered wrapped gifts for Hodo. Nazmi apparently had intended to ship them. Hodo did not live long after her son's murder. Gloria recalled Awad telling her, "Mother was so upset over Nazmi's death, she died."

Noura's paternal family in Lebanon—three uncles, Awad, Ramzi Chafic Hassanieh, Naji Chafic Hassanieh; and two aunts, Aida Hassanieh and Naziha Hassanieh—are perhaps unaware of what became of their niece and their mother's first grandchild. Gloria does not know if they knew of Jennifer's death and Noura's subsequent arrest.

While Gloria was visiting Noura at the Shelby County Jail, or Jail East, as the women's facility is known, Noura told Gloria, "If my daddy was alive I wouldn't have been arrested."

Gloria said she replied, "I know he wouldn't have let you sit in jail for three years."

Nazmi's estate remained a nagging problem for Jennifer. Creditors' claims outweighed its value, and so far she only had been able to procure a clear title to one of the minivans, though she preferred driving the Mercedes. Technically what did not belong to creditors belonged to Noura, who mistakenly believed there was a small fortune in her father's vehicles and business. Regardless of the facts Jennifer produced, she could not convince Noura otherwise. Jennifer even asked a friend to review Nazmi's so-called business records. What a joke! A bunch of receipts stuffed haphazardly into a box. No one could make sense of it.

But through Noura's eyes it looked quite different. For over a year she had fantasized about what was hers since her father's death. Jennifer had been able to stall her, but now, with her eighteenth birthday, she knew Noura would really push the matter. With all the problems she had, the thought of Noura on her own with any kind of cash flow meant more trouble than Jennifer could face.

Jennifer's brother Eric was among those privy to the tumultuous tides facing Jennifer as Noura's behavior worsened and her fixation on money intensified. Eric was a frequent dinner guest, joining them two or three times a week. He was there before Noura's birthday when the conversation took the unhappy turn toward Noura's father's money. That spring Noura was desperate for independence. She wouldn't have to ask her mom for a thing! She'd have her own income and freedom. What she coveted was about to materialize.

Hence Jennifer's pronouncement at dinner that night ignited a firestorm. She informed Noura that should there be any proceeds from the estate, they would be used for her college fund, and, should Noura choose not to attend college, Jennifer would keep the money as unpaid back child support. This idea infuriated Noura. Her mom knew college wasn't something she cared about, certainly not anytime soon. Good grief, she hadn't even finished high school! This was another attempt to control her; to keep what was rightfully hers.

Eric remembered Noura challenging her mother, arguing that the money was hers, and she could use it however she wished. Noura stormed away from the table in a fury. It was one of those flareups that would not easily be tamped down.

Jennifer neighbors, the Cockes, were folks she felt comfortable asking for help, as she had Memorial Day weekend when they kept an eye on her house. Jennifer especially appreciated Sheila's good sense. She listened well and held her opinions and advice until asked, which were qualities Jennifer was coming to appreciate more and more. Jennifer had confided in Sheila so she was aware of Jennifer's anxiety about Noura's approaching birthday. "There was a great deal of concern about Noura turning eighteen," Sheila said.

The worries Jennifer had shared with Sheila manifested themselves during the spring of 2005. Around 9:30 one evening as she took her dog on the last walk of the day, Sheila saw Jennifer and Noura in the driveway, walking toward the house. They were arguing.

"Just give me the fucking money! Just give me the fucking money!" Noura demanded. Jennifer entreated Noura to be quiet and go inside where they privately could talk, "Shhhh. Let's get inside."

Later that same spring, Sheila heard a similar argument about the money. "It's my money! Give me the money! I want my money!" Sheila testified, adding that her own intonation was not exactly right, "Noura's voice had a little more rage to it."

Jennifer replied, "I will. I will."

Jennifer Jackson was an attractive, thirty-nine-year-old bond trader and single mother found stabbed more than fifty times in her East Memphis home.

The top of Jennifer's armoire displays Noura's childhood photographs and a photograph of mother and daughter.

"My sister," Grace France said of Jennifer, "was not the best housekeeper." In the midst of the sunroom clutter, Jennifer's brother Eric discovered her wallet in an uncovered plastic bin.

A party-inspired, cell phone photo of Noura and three friends on the eve of Jennifer's death became a key piece of evidence for the prosecution.

The Jackson family frequently vacationed in Florida. This photo from Disney World—Noura on the left, Jennifer, and a friend of Noura's—occurred before Jennifer and Noura's relationship soured.

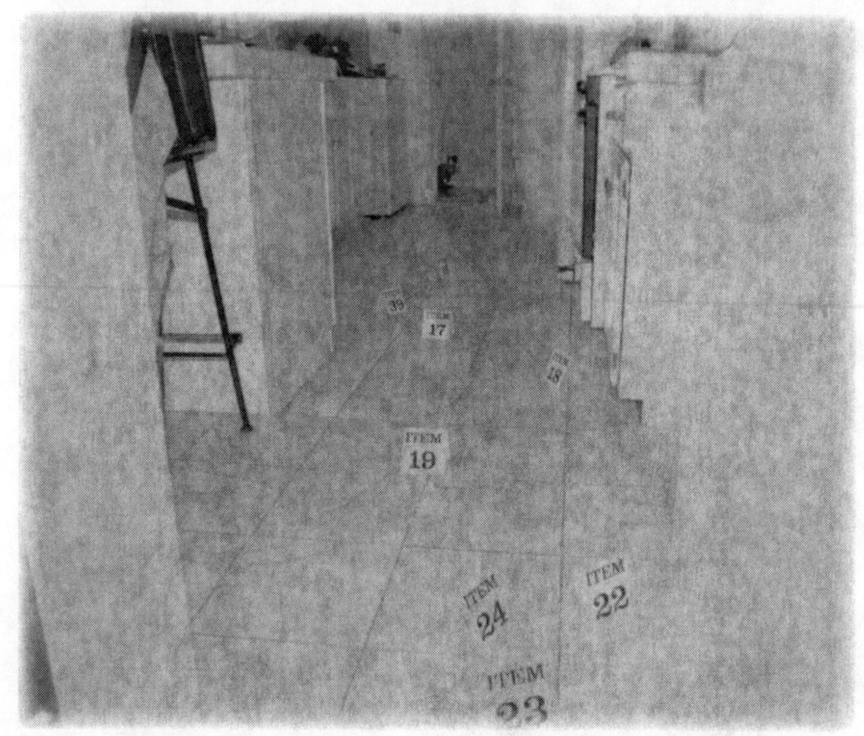

Noura's new kitten is evident toward the top of this crime scene photograph. Noura's attorney voiced concern over the integrity of an investigation that allowed the cat to prowl the crime scene.

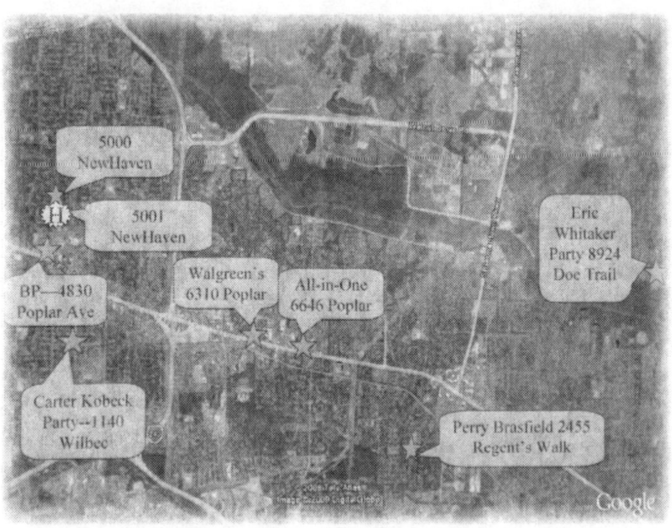

A map marks Noura's travels on June 4 and 5 primarily along the Poplar Corridor, a major east-west thoroughfare.

The Jackson home at 5001 New Haven resembled many East Memphis homes built in the mid-1950s. The one-level ranch was a solid home in a nice area though one side of the house ran parallel to a busy street.

Part II

The bloody trail from the master bedroom continued all the way to the front porch.

Wicker Basket

"She's been murdered! She's been murdered!"—Joe Cocke

"It was odd there was a basket over the body. It seemed weird to me."—Paramedic Michelle Hulbert

Jennifer and Noura's neighbors, Joe and Rachael Cocke, are a study in contrasts. Joe is tall with dark hair and intense eyes who has an edgy, anxious quality about him. Rachael's personality engages quickly with people, and she emanates goodwill and calmness—an almost impossible-to-imagine calmness. These qualities—Joe's quickness and Rachael's steadiness—would be important to their accidental roles in the discovery of Jennifer's body.

That Saturday the Cockes babysat their young nephew who spent the night them. He slept in a crib in a front bedroom, and through the baby monitor, Rachael was listening to the eleven-month-old messing around, making noises, and fussing a little. It was 5:00 a.m. or within the first few minutes of 5:00 a.m. Sunday. Suddenly those endearing baby sounds could not be heard over the shouting and banging on the front door. Rachael ran to the door and heard someone screaming, “My mom, my mom! Someone is breaking into my house!” Rachael called out for her husband.

Joe, who had been sleeping, immediately was alert and alarmed by what his wife was saying. He grabbed his pistol and went to the front door. There stood Noura screaming. Joe rushed to Noura’s aid. It was still semidark when, armed with his pistol, Joe ran across the street with Noura. At the same time, Rachael called 911 from their home phone.

Joe stopped outside the house to put a bullet in the pistol’s chamber. By habit Noura used the front door—the door she had a key to—to come and go from her house, and the morning of June 5 was no exception. Joe remarked later that he didn’t understand why Noura hurried in her house ahead of him and went straight to the sunroom. He entered cautiously with his gun drawn. The loaded weapon made him nervous, and he was afraid he might shoot someone, like himself or Jennifer. He said he was looking everywhere for moving bodies. The shadowy light in the house heightened Joe’s apprehension. When he was confident there were no intruders in the house, he asked Noura where her mother was. “She’s in her room,” was the response. Noura had been in her mother’s room before she ran to the Cocke’s house.

He made his way down the hall to Jennifer’s bedroom. First he saw the bed soaked in blood. Then he saw Jennifer covered in blood lying nude on the floor. “I went back to the bedroom and saw the bed covered in blood. [Jennifer] was murdered. She had blood all over her. She was dead."

Joe bolted out of the room, out of the house, and ran back home, shouting to Rachael, "She's been murdered! She's been murdered!"

Jennifer's attacker killed her in a vicious knife attack. Her body lay slightly curled on the floor parallel to the bed's footboard with her feet just touching the left bedpost and her head closer to the right bedpost and bedroom door. Her right arm was draped across her body just under her chest. Her open eyes reflected shock and outrage. Someone snatched her from her sleep, took her life, and forever stole her privacy.

Though short in stature, especially in relation to her husband, Rachael took control of the situation, trying to calm Joe and find out if he was sure Jennifer was dead. Her husband, she said, "freaks out from blood."

She asked Joe repeatedly, "Was Jennifer still breathing? Is she alive?" And then told Joe "We have to check." While she volleyed questions at him, Rachael was still on the phone with a 911 operator. She passed the phone to her mother-in-law, Sheila, and Rachael and Joe hurried back across the street.

Noura also had placed a call to 911 from the land line in the sunroom. In tones that raced from frantic to hysterical—"Oh my God. Oh my God"—Noura entreated the dispatcher to "Please help me. Someone broke into my house! My mom is bleeding!"

Asked if anyone was shot she said, "No. No one was shot. But there is blood everywhere, and she's not breathing! She's not breathing! She's not breathing!"

Noura coherently told the dispatcher that her mother was thirty-nine years old. Asked if Noura saw what happened, she said, "No, I just got home." She stated that someone broke into the house. "I went to go get my kitten in the kitchen, and there was glass everywhere. . . . Please send an ambulance."

Noura was having trouble breathing and her voice alternated from shrieks to almost whimpers. Upset by the dispatcher's incessant questions, Noura eventually shouted, "I want someone to help me right now!"

While Joe described Jennifer as a friend and neighbor, Rachael said she didn't know Noura at all; at most she might have waved to her across the street. When Joe reentered the Jackson home with Rachael, they found Noura sitting on the sunroom floor, rocking and talking to 911. Rachael took the phone from Noura and the dispatcher asked Rachael if she knew CPR. She said she didn't and the operator said she would talk her through it. Not knowing the home's layout, Rachael followed the bloody footprints down the hall to the bedroom where a faint light burned. Rachael's conversation with 911 was encumbered because she was on a land line. That necessitated running back and forth between Jennifer and the sunroom.

"Are you right by her now?" the operator asked.

"Yes," Rachael said.

She instructed Rachael to lie Jennifer flat on her back and remove anything from behind her head.

"Do you want to try CPR?"

Rachael approached Jennifer and didn't see any movement from the waist up. She looked at the body and said there was no use.

"She's not alive. There's no pulse, and she's not breathing." After repeated efforts by the dispatcher to get her to try CPR, Rachael said, "I can't ma'am . . . she's been there a long time it looks like." She saw no movement and Jennifer's face was "fixed."

While Rachael talked with 911, Joe and Noura stayed near the foyer and kitchen. At one point Noura tried to go to her mother, but Joe bumped her back into the kitchen where the floor was littered with broken glass. All the time Noura was asking, "Is she dead? Is she dead? Is she dead?"

When Rachael returned to the sunroom having determined there was nothing she could do for Jennifer, Noura had resumed her rocking and wailing. In the gloomy twilight, the reality of what had happened down the hall settled around them. Joe had not gone with his wife to Jennifer's bedroom but had remained in the foyer. "I didn't want to go in that room again. And I didn't go back in that room again," he said.

Rachael turned her attention to Noura and noticed that there was no blood on her. Noura alternated between screaming and hysteria, and though she was crying, there were no actual tears. Mostly she noticed Noura was very sweaty.

Noura wailed, "What will I do? I just lost my dad. Why is this happening to me?" Rachael sat beside her on the floor, trying to console her as they waited for police and paramedics to arrive. Rachael estimated that no more than five minutes elapsed between the time Noura banged on their front door and they returned home. Rachael and Joe wasted no time leaving the Jackson house once the police arrived.

Memphis Police Officer Russell Tankersley remembers the morning of June 5 as unseasonably hot and sticky; the temperature was already ninety or ninety-five degrees when he arrived at the Jackson residence about 5:15 a.m. At almost the same exact time his partner pulled up in his vehicle in response to a call about a possible robbery. The house was very dark with only a porch light burning and a few lamps on inside. Noura appeared outside screaming that something "was wrong" with her mom.

Tankersley entered the house with a flashlight and his weapon drawn—"flashlight out in his left hand, gun in right hand with right wrist crossing over left wrist." Inside, he noticed blood on the floor and broken glass in the kitchen. While he followed procedure to clear the house, Noura came back inside and told him her mother "was in the back." Then she again started yelling, "My mom, my mom!" and, as she had done with Joe Cocke, tried to go back to Jennifer's bedroom.

Tankersley asked his partner to get Noura out of the house—"to keep her from getting hurt; and, if there was someone in the house, he didn't want their position revealed"—and he made his way down the hall. Walking slowly into the dark bedroom he saw blood on the floor, blood on the bed, an arm, and then Jennifer's body. He quickly backed out having only gone about a foot into the room.

When he had cleared the house to wait for paramedics, he observed Noura more closely. She was wearing a blue-jean skirt and a gray long-sleeved fleece or sweatshirt. In the already sweltering morning, the gray hoodie sent up a "little red flag" for the officer. (Interestingly, no one ever considered that Noura might be in shock.) "Though we had not questioned her beyond asking her name, "Tankersley said, "she kept telling us she was tired and just wanted to go to sleep."

Moments later Michelle Hulbert, a Memphis Fire Department paramedic arrived from her station on Mendenhall near Sanderlin, a few short blocks from the Jackson home. Hulbert was the first medical responder to enter Jennifer's bedroom—"an obvious crime scene"—and confirmed Rachael's assessment. In order for her to examine the body, Hulbert removed a basket that was covering the victim's face and head. "It was odd there was a basket over the body. It seemed weird to me," she said.

The brown, wicker basket was turned open side down and covered Jennifer's face, head, and neck.

Hulbert's examination noted Jennifer's mouth was full of blood. She placed a cardiac monitor on Jennifer's cheek to check for electrical activity in her heart, but there was none. Hulbert said she stopped counting stab wounds at fifteen. (The prosecution publicly said Jennifer was stabbed or cut more than fifty times, though it actually was closer to seventy. According to the medical examiner, cuts are more long than deep, while stab wounds are deeper into the body.) Hulbert didn't observe rigor in Jennifer's wrist, and though she did not take a core temperature, she described Jennifer's body temperature "as cool not cold." At 5:18 a.m. Hulbert pronounced "a dead body."

Hulbert found Noura sitting outside on the curb. Noura gave Hulbert her mother's name and other information, and asked her for a cigarette. When a police officer approached and asked about Jennifer's boyfriend, Mark Irvin, Noura said, "He's an asshole but even *he* wouldn't do something like that."

It didn't take long for detectives to start wondering why Noura told 911 that her mom hadn't been shot. How could she be sure? The room was dimly lit, and Jennifer's body was completely covered in blood. "No," Detective Helldorfer said, "there's no way in the world she could have known that."

The wicker basket viscerally affected almost everyone involved with the investigation and trial. There was a flurry of questions from the jury about the basket. What type of basket was it? Where was it placed on Jennifer's body? And a final question for Judge Craft, "Had anyone prior to Michelle Hulbert mentioned the basket?" Since those witnesses—Joe and Rachael Cocke and Officer Russell Tankersley— already had been dismissed, the question went unanswered.

When Noura described finding her mother in her witness statement, she said, "So I walked into my mom's room and I took the basket off her head." The prosecution called the wicker basket a "'wall of shame. 'Don't look at me mom. Don't look at me while I clean this up.'"

For the jury, the wicker basket's significance was that Jennifer was killed by someone she knew. "You just don't want to look at her face," a juror surmised. "You just don't want to look in those eyes. And you don't want to shut them—you don't want to touch it—so you put something over it. And you know if someone else had done that, they just would have walked away. You don't have that connection with the eyes. You just don't."

Ryan Young, who was accused and convicted of matricide in Florida in 2009, wanted to avoid his mother's gaze. Donna Young had been suffocated in her bed and was discovered by her son. "First [Ryan] told the detective he didn't put the pillow on his mother's face and said it was like that when he got to the house. Then he said he put it there because he didn't want to see her dead. Then he said he put it there and pressed down because he was angry at her about her disappointment in his homosexuality."

After repeating many times that he hadn't "meant to [kill her]," Ryan added, "I was happy she was dead."[13]

The confusion with the wicker basket is threefold. Noura told Officer Justice that when she arrived home the basket was covering her mother's face and Noura removed it. She then ran across the street to the Cockes who came to her aid and tried to help Jennifer. They did not see a basket. Moments later when Michelle Hulbert arrived, she had to remove the basket to examine Jennifer. So what happened between Noura's initial discovery—before she fled across the street to get the Cockes—and Hulbert's examination? How and why was the wicker basket *again* covering Jennifer's face and upper body? Joe and Rachael Cocke were adamant they never saw a basket over Jennifer's face that morning. "Joe and I did not touch anything in the house, with the exception of the telephone and the front door," Rachael said. Nor did Joe or Noura accompany Rachael, as she conferred with 911, down the hall to Jennifer's bedroom.

Rachael said on the morning of June 5 that they eventually walked outside to wait for the police. "There were times that I can't recall where Noura was, and she was the last to exit the house when emergency personnel arrived. It is our opinion [Rachael and Joe's] that Noura must have placed the basket over Jennifer's face before the paramedics went in."

---

[13] Michael Kruse, "Ryan Young's Own Statements Turn Against Him in Matricide Trial," *Tampa Bay Times*, 22 January 2009.

A Circus

"This was out East. Good-looking, white woman murdered in a nice neighborhood. We knew it was going to be high profile; we just didn't know how high it was going to go."—Detective Helldorfer

"Is all of this all going to be on the news?"—Noura to Patti Masterson

Genevieve Dix was among the first of family and friends to arrive at 5001 New Haven on the hot and steamy morning of June 5. Jennifer's cousin, Randolph Reeves, called Dix about 7:00 a.m., and she arrived shortly after to a scene described as "a circus." Officially twenty-two individuals entered the crime scene—between 5:00 a.m. and noon. Even more patrolled outside. Dix was forced to park her car several houses down from Jennifer and Noura's home. Uniformed police officers and investigators covered the house and perimeter. When Dix was able to get closer, she encountered Randolph and his partner, Tony. (Randolph would tell Bill Shelton, Jennifer's former boyfriend, "We suspected Noura from day one.")

They shared a comforting hug. Then Dix made her way toward Noura who was sitting on the grass.

Dix, an attorney specializing in domestic relations and real estate since 1976, was a very emotional, dramatic, and, some might say, practiced trial witness. She managed to share her opinions effectively during her testimony: casting doubt on Noura's emotional reaction to her mother's murder; Noura's unwillingness to help investigators; and also Noura's unsubstantial account of her evening and early morning hours.

Dix recalled saying to Noura, "Oh, baby, this is terrible!" to which Noura replied, "Who will come to my graduation?" Dix added, "I thought this was an odd statement." Dix thought the odd statement matched Noura's unstylish outfit. It certainly wasn't one of Noura's just home from partying outfits. A short, light-wash denim skirt (she'd worn a dark-wash denim skirt at Perry's house the night before), New Balance tennis shoes, and a gray hoodie (described also as a fleece sweatshirt) pulled down to her knuckles. Noura usually "dressed in really lovely clothes . . . whatever was fashionable," Dix said. When Dix hugged her, Noura did not reciprocate but kept her arms to her side.

"Noura's hair didn't smell like smoke. It was very fresh smelling, fresh and sweet. I was surprised because Noura is a smoker. I remember thinking, 'You're so pretty when you don't wear makeup.'" Noura usually wore heavy black eye makeup, and there were no makeup smears or traces of makeup from the night before.

Dix's friendship with Jennifer, whom she described as her best friend, began in 1993 when Noura was six years old and her own daughter five. "Noura," she said, "is an extremely bright individual. I've known her since she was in kindergarten." Noura and her daughter had grown up together. Dix and Jennifer saw each other frequently, including Sundays at church. Not too long after she met Jennifer, she accompanied her to a legal proceeding involving Nazmi when he failed to pay child support.

A good deal of confusion surrounded Noura's interactions that morning with her mother's friend. So much so that it became an issue in her Criminal Court of Appeals motion. Noura's attorneys argued in her appeal "that she would not have signed the consent to search unless she believed that Ms. Dix was functioning as her attorney."

Genevieve Dix testified she made it clear she was not acting as Noura's attorney. According to her testimony, an officer approached Dix to say that Noura wanted to speak with her.

> When the officer came over and said, "Who are you?" I told him.
>
> Then he took me over to where [Noura] was and he had handed her the consent form.
>
> And he said, "[Noura] wants to talk to you about this."

> I said, "I don't represent her. I'm not a criminal attorney. What is that?"
>
> And he said, "That's a consent to search."
>
> I said, "I've never seen one. I don't do criminal law."
>
> He said, "Well, she wants to talk to you."
>
> And so, I walked with Noura over to the driveway area and I said . . . "I can't represent you."

No one else will ever know exactly what words were exchanged between the two when they talked in private Sunday morning. Dix maintained she was there as Jennifer's friend, not to give Noura legal counsel. She said she did tell Noura she had the right to an attorney.

When the officers kept coming at her with consent forms to sign, Noura singled out Genevieve because she knew she was a lawyer. Noura said she trusted Dix's advice as an attorney. For her part, Genevieve became more and more upset with Noura when she persisted to question whether or not she should sign the forms. She kept asking Dix if they could "get in my car." Noura asked about the car "five or six times" until "I became angry and asked 'What in the world's in your car that you're so worried about it, and your mother's lying dead in there and they need to investigate?'

"She wanted to know if they could get in her Jeep, and I said, 'Your mother's in there dead not forty feet away. Don't you want to help the [police]?'" Noura said she had a bong pipe in the car. Dix was incredulous, telling Noura she didn't believe the police would care much about the bong given the slaying. At 7:53 a.m. Noura signed consent forms allowing police to search the house, premises, and vehicles. The vehicle search, according to Sergeant Helldorfer, amounted to him looking inside for blood and at various items of clothing.

Dix questioned why the police even sought Noura's consent since the house and cars belonged to her mother. While at the scene Dix began her own interrogation of Noura, asking her where she'd been the night before.

"Mom went to a wedding last night and called me around 11:30 or 12:00 and wanted me to come home too. But you know me. I came home about four o'clock."

Defense attorney Corder returned to Dix in her closing argument, "Unwittingly, Genevieve Dix turns out to be one of the best witnesses for the defense. No one who's just killed their mother would be worried about a bong in her car." Corder also lamented the prosecution's tactic of character assassination; one witness after another recalled Noura's drug use or fights with her mother. "To put the character of a child on trial, and prohibit the inquiring into the character of the people condemning and demonizing her, I don't think is a fair playing field," Corder said.

Dix would later read the victim impact statement on behalf of the Jackson siblings, and when she stepped down from the witness stand, she and Jennifer's sister, Grace, exchanged broad smiles.

Another of Jennifer's friends, Patti Masterson, who was her real estate agent when she purchased her home, arrived around 9:30 that morning and spent several hours observing 5001 New Haven from a neighbor's yard. Her vigil didn't end until 4:00 p.m. when her friend's body was removed from the house.

About thirty minutes after she arrived, she saw Noura walking along the sidewalk by herself. Masterson said she had to ask herself what she would do when she saw Noura. She finally walked over, and she and Noura hugged each other.

Masterson, like Dix, told Noura how sorry she was about her mother.

Noura asked, "Is all of this going to be on the news?"

She told her "Yes, Noura, this is a very, very big deal."

Masterson also noticed Noura's outfit. It was midmorning and the sweltering temperatures had been climbing. The high that day reached ninety-four degrees, and the night's low, seventy-four degrees, brought no relief. Masterson said, "You must be very hot, wearing those two long-sleeved shirts." Noura pulled the sweatshirt off and threw it on the ground and walked away from Masterson. Some of Noura's friends who also were nearby offered to give it back to Noura.

Masterson said, "No, I'll give it to the detectives. And I did."

She did not interact with Noura ever again.

The gray hoodie, like Noura's gold sandals with the sparkly rhinestones, became a focal point for the investigation. The Tennessee Bureau of Investigation (TBI) processed the hoodie twice. It was examined on June 14, 2005, found to be free of blood, and stored in the property room. Then investigators wanted TBI to look specifically at the left sleeve. During the second TBI examination on August 15, 2005, they found a napkin in the through-and-through pocket. The napkin, with what looked like blood on it, was sent separately for testing. It matched Noura's blood DNA.

The juror who came to be known as Question Man was puzzled by the subsequent discovery of the napkin and asked about timing. DNA expert and TBI agent Qadriyyah Debnam said she examined the sweatshirt in June and did not see any blood nor did she find the napkin. She received the napkin for testing August 17, 2005. Debman also tested Noura's cigarette pack, lighter, and gold sandals. All were negative for blood.

In her witness statement to Officer Connie Justice, Noura said she had not been home the night of June 4. That made the discovery of her gold sandals under a table in the foyer difficult to explain. Several witnesses, including Perry, recalled Noura wearing the sandals at Carter's house Saturday night. Day five of the trial included a brief appearance by Officer Sam Blue, a crime scene investigator. With Officer Blue's testimony, three photographs of the sandals became evidential exhibits.

"In my mind," Detective Helldorfer said in an interview, "a key thing was also the picture that was on the cell phone from the friend showing what she [Noura] was wearing the night before. When I saw the gold slippers in the house. . . . If she'd never been in the house, how did they get there? To me the slippers inside the house said she was there."

Meanwhile, word of Jennifer's death spread rapidly to Noura's circle of friends. Perry's mother received a phone call about Jennifer's death, and Perry and Joey (now both back at Perry's after spending the night at Sophie's) immediately headed to Noura's home on New Haven. Perry remembers her just walking her dog on the sidewalk. He hugged Noura and asked her how she was doing. "Are you okay? What's going on here?" Shortly thereafter he went to police headquarters to give his first statement. (He would give a second statement to police that included the visit to Sophie's which he had omitted the first time.)

When Perry asked Noura about the cut on her hand, she said she had been chasing her kitten in the house, tripped, and cut her hand on some broken glass. Perry was surprised to learn she had a kitten.

When Genevieve Dix and Perry had an opportunity to talk that morning, Dix discovered he had received a different version of events from Noura. Dix demanded Perry tell the police what Noura told him. He said Noura had called him around 12:30 and said she was at home. Dix immediately confronted Noura about the discrepancy, asking her why Noura told her 4:00 a.m. and Perry something different? Noura said she actually drove by her house and saw the lights were out. She then drove on to a boy's house and smoked pot in the driveway until 4:00 a.m. She told her aunt Grace she was with "Chris," a name completely new to everyone, and that she didn't tell anyone because Perry "hates him."

Neighbor Sheila Cocke crossed the street that Sunday morning in her wheelchair (she had a broken foot at the time), to see to Noura and be as maternal as possible, even though she was "horrified" by what her son and daughter-in-law had witnessed in Jennifer Jackson's bedroom.

"I was trying to give all the comfort to her I possibly could," Cocke said. Different officers kept approaching Noura, asking her where she had been during the murder, "and she never gave the same answer twice. . . . I thought, oh, my goodness. Oh, my goodness . . . you better be able to come front and center with where you were." This led Cocke to be concerned about statements she was hearing from Noura.

A juror felt Sheila Cocke's inclination—to first protect Noura and then worry about her inconsistent statements—was pure instinct. "When she said, 'Oh my God, Noura. You've got to be on your game with this' or something like that. That is a woman whose instinct right then kicked in. If you were to talk with her, she'd tell you that at that point the hair on the back of her neck went up."

Dix and Perry's early conversations with Noura would be the first of her many revised accounts. Noura chose not to reveal her exact whereabouts during the early morning hours of June 5. And in addition to telling Perry she cut her hand chasing her new kitten in the house, she gave at least four other stories accounting for the small cut on the back of her left hand between her thumb and index finger.

Garden of Everlasting Hope

"He gathers the lambs in His arms and carries them close to His heart."—Isaiah 40:11

In Noura's constellation of potential mother figures, Regina Hunt's placement was among the most complex. She, unlike the other women, assumed a more peer-like role. She shared confidences with Noura and saw her on a regular basis. Hunt, a thin, pensive woman with vividly bright, blonde hair, appeared captivated by the teenage drama around her. She owned a sandwich shop in East Memphis, Roly Poly, where she employed Noura's friends, Clark Schifani and Joey McGoff.

Located less than a mile from the Jackson home, Roly Poly became a hangout for the group. Often during school hours Noura and assorted friends would show up at the restaurant. Noura's excuses were that she didn't like school, or she was sick, and though Hunt discouraged this behavior, it had little impact. "It was probably once a week that she would be in Roly, if not more," Hunt said. She said she would fix Noura a sandwich and try to talk her into going to school. The two also discussed the Gateway home-school program.

After the Memorial Day weekend trip to Florida, Noura ranted to Hunt about the restraining order against Perry and the fact that Jennifer was drug testing her. Perry and Clark were at the restaurant at the time. Hunt said she was used to such eruptions from Noura, citing her "disrespectful" way of talking to Jennifer. On a number of occasions Hunt said she admonished Noura for speaking in such an "ugly" manner to her mother.

Hunt's own characterization of her relationship with Noura vacillated from scolding adult to solicitous friend. She was the person who stepped in to care for Noura during the day and evening of June 5; she even invited several of Noura's friends to her home as well.

The dynamics between the two leave much to be sorted. Noura was a third grader when Hunt met her and Jennifer at Holy Communion Church. She was Noura's Sunday school teacher, though she referred to herself as Noura's godmother (in actuality Noura's godmother is Jennifer's friend, Debra Mays). One of Hunt's children went to St. George's with Noura. Clearly, she was someone with whom Noura was comfortable sharing her confidences. She complained to Hunt that when she spoke with her aunts "[t]he big issue was always money."

Noura felt her aunts were keeping her money from her—that her father's cars were hers, and the money was hers. She insisted they wanted her to rent a cheap apartment and would not give her what was rightfully hers. They planned to hold her money, so Noura could go to school and get a job, but Noura said she wasn't going to do either. By her own admission, Hunt disclosed going through Noura's purse—"just being nosy"—and finding twelve to twenty tablets with "little specks on them" in a prescription bottle labeled Concerta. When Hunt took them to a Walgreen's pharmacist for identification, he described the pills as street-grade hydrocodone (though Concerta is an amphetamine stimulant prescribed for Attention Deficit Hyperactivity Disorder.)

By the time Hunt arrived at New Haven on June 5. Noura had returned from her trip to police headquarters downtown where she gave a witness statement, DNA samples, and was photographed. She hugged Noura, and Noura told her she wanted "to get out of there." Sophie remembered Noura sitting in the front passenger seat of Hunt's car with a Ziploc bag four or five inches high filled with "very, very many Lortabs. I thought it was a large amount (sic). I couldn't believe it," Sophie said. Most would agree it was a strange time for Noura to display prescription pills when her mother's body was still in their house. Those with Noura in and around Hunt's car knew Noura and Jennifer had argued often about drugs. Hunt said Noura told her she was uncomfortable with her mother's friends who were standing across the street from the house. She insisted Hunt take her away from there.

Hunt was concerned that Noura needed something to eat and took her to Roly Poly where Perry and a few other friends had gathered. Agitated and upset, Noura again urged Hunt to get her out of there, saying she didn't want to see them. Instead, they went in a back entrance to Hunt's office, and Noura had a sandwich. It was now early afternoon and Noura wanted her belongings. Hunt drove her back to New Haven where Noura asked a police officer if she could get her purse and cell phone that were in her bedroom and a bag of clothes out of her Jeep. (Noura's cell phone was visually inspected for blood at the time but never sent away for testing. Call history showed the last number dialed from her cell phone was to Andrew Hammack.)

With the officer's permission, she got her things, and Hunt took her to Caroline Giovannetti's house. Caroline was a friend of Noura's. Some of Noura's friends were there, but this time Noura appeared calm around them. Noura showered and borrowed enough clothes for a few days from Caroline. The friends talked in the kitchen, and at one point Joey and Noura disappeared from the front of the house only to return, according to Hunt, smelling like marijuana.

The rotating madness of June 5 continued with a trip to the cemetery. Hunt felt Noura needed the comfort of her friends (even though at her restaurant Noura refused to see them). From Caroline's they headed for Hunt's house in what was now a caravan of three cars. Noura asked Hunt if they could stop at Anna's grave at Memorial Park Cemetery. There, Noura's emotional outburst was unlike anything that occurred at New Haven.

Memorial Park is incongruously located at 5668 Poplar Avenue in East Memphis, one Memphis's busiest streets, with nearby interstate access. A vast, wooded, rolling expanse of approximately fifty-four acres, the cemetery is divided by named sections. In early June the grass is full and green and the gravesites mostly well tended by family and friends. If the connotations of death could be banished by a word, calling the cemetery a "park" attempts to serve that purpose.

Anna's grave is situated near a rise in the section called Garden of Everlasting Hope. Her marker, "Anna Caroline Menkel, 9/27/1987-1/23/2005, Beloved Daughter, Sister, Granddaughter and Friend," also is inscribed with a passage from Isaiah. Standing at Anna's graveside, Noura seemed at last to feel the finality and wreckage of all that had occurred. Loss, loss, loss. Her best friend, her dad, her mom. For the first time that anyone had seen, she really cried, sobbed, saying, "I want to be with Anna and my mother."

Meanwhile, Hunt had returned to her car to wait for Noura when one of Noura's friends approached her and asked if Noura could smoke some weed at the gravesite. Hunt registered neither surprise nor disapproval, saying merely, "No, it's getting late and we need to go."

From about 4:00 p.m. until around 11:00 p.m., Noura's friends stayed at Hunt's home. Hunt ordered pizza, and as the night continued, the group grew to twenty or so people. Sophie remembered Noura as "not very emotional. Just upset but not overly upset." It was then she noticed the small, white bandage on Noura's left hand.

According to Hunt, Noura's requests were stunningly odd. Shopping? Tanning? Movies? A party? Those didn't seem to be activities a grieving daughter would even think about let alone suggest. Hunt continued to hold the line, insisting that behavior would be inappropriate. At one point the conversation turned to Noura's cut. Noura said she cut herself on a beer bottle at Italian Fest. "Caroline," she said, "you saw me, you saw how drunk I was." Caroline, however, was babysitting Saturday night and saw Noura—not particularly drunk—at the festival Friday night. Hunt started a mental catalogue of Noura's answers and explanations. Soon she would drill Noura on these discrepancies until a second breakdown occurred.

If Hunt was intent on finding Noura in a lie, she had to look no further than the prescription bottle she took to Walgreens. She asked Noura about the bottle of pills in her purse with the name "Robert" on them. Noura said a doctor had prescribed them for her for cramps. Hunt, incredulous, told Noura to "quit filling [me] full of crap and tell [me] where [you] got them." She pressed until Noura confessed she bought the pills from someone at Ridgeway High School.

Now Hunt insisted Noura tell her "everything you did on Saturday." Noura's description of the postmidnight hours especially was troubling. Noura told her she drove by New Haven, saw the lights were out, and kept on driving. Then the account changed. She said she *did* go home and snuck out in the early morning hours.

Noura not only found herself fending off Hunt's questions, but she also was taking phone calls from detectives. (As early as Monday, June 6, the Memphis Police Department had requested Noura's cell phone records.) They called to speak with Noura while she was at Hunt's home. The phone call with detectives rattled Noura. She asked Hunt if she was a suspect. Hunt told her everyone was a suspect. "I love my mother," Noura said. "I hug my mother. I touch my mother. I'm all over my mother." When Hunt assured her they would find the murderer Noura was angered, saying tersely, "They never found out who killed my father."

Noura's bizarre requests continued on Monday, and when Hunt refused to accommodate her, Noura called Kathy Menkel, Anna's mother, to pick her up. Noura spent the day and night of June 6 at the Menkel home. Menkel was another mother figure for Noura. In fact, their friendship really developed after Anna's death.

Ironically, Menkel's conversation with detectives on June 17 after driving Noura's Jeep Cherokee probably had more to do with making the state's case against Noura than any other development. When Menkel drove Noura's Jeep from her house to the New Haven home on June 9—Noura had at this point been admitted to Charter Lakeside Hospital for her emotional state—she noticed a Walgreens drug store bag in the back of the Jeep. Inside she saw medical tape, an empty New Skin box, and other wound-care supplies. Noura told Menkel when she asked about the Walgreens bag that her mother had bought the items for her after she cut her hand at the Italian Fest on June 3.

The same day as their interview with Menkel, June 17, detectives pulled up at the Jackson home, saw the Jeep in the driveway, and the Walgreens bag in "clear view." With that as probable cause, they called for a tow and impounded the vehicle to be thoroughly processed. Lawrence Buser reported for *The Commercial Appeal* that "They also seized from her 1998 Jeep Grand Cherokee a stained bath wrap, a towel embroidered with 'Noura Grace,' two plastic Walgreens bags, an empty box of Skin Shield Liquid Bandage, one Q-tip, Nexcare liquid bandage drops, a stained paper towel and two floor mats."

In her motion to suppress, defense attorney Corder vehemently challenged the search of Noura's Jeep that day, stating that the police were on Noura's property June 17, 2005, without her permission and that her Fourth Amendment protection—a legitimate expectation of privacy—was violated. Questioning why the police needed Noura to sign a search consent for her vehicle on June 5 but did not on June 17, Corder asked, "Why on June 17 did she no longer have her Fourth Amendment right? What happened between June 5 and June 17?"

Judge Craft denied the motion on April 30, 2008, and the State Criminal Court of Appeals affirmed his ruling. Had Corder squelched the admittance of the Walgreens' evidence, the prosecution would have lost a damning piece of its case.

Tuesday morning June 7 when she picked Noura up from the Menkels, Regina Hunt persisted, even intensified, her line of questioning. Driving on Poplar with Noura in the passenger seat, Hunt revisited the cut. Noura said her kitten was stuck in the garage, and she cut her hand freeing it. Confronted with the two differing versions, Noura began sobbing a second time, saying over and over, "I want to kill myself! I want to kill myself!" Hunt was so alarmed by Noura's emotional volatility that she took her to see a doctor. He spoke privately with Noura and then told Hunt that Noura needed to be hospitalized. According to the doctor, "She wanted to kill herself and had some drug issues."

Noura's possible suicidal tendencies were threaded throughout testimony and in comments posted online like this from day five of the trial.

> **NoName2** Says: Bull. She didn't just want to kill herself . . . she tried. I was once very close to Noura and after the murder of her mother she tried to throw herself out of a moving vehicle in germantown. A lot of what will make some of yall believe she had something to do with the murder hasn't even come out yet. You just wait. There is a lot more to come. Your jaws will drop.

Perhaps because Hunt's sandwich shop was a magnet for many of the trial's young witnesses, and she herself was well known to them, or for the inexplicable reasons that some witnesses fascinate more than others, Regina Hunt's testimony evoked a flurry of anonymous newspaper postings. Hunt was depicted as a "cougar" who bought alcohol for underage employees, but others begged to differ.

> **Splicka** Says: . . . she should stick to what she knows best, being a cougarific scandalizer

with fake hair, pounds of make up and emotionally unstable behavior, yea thats right lady.

vipmel Says: That woman is a wack job. She got kicked out of Holy Communion for "inappropriate" behavior with teenage boys.

becky Says: I have grown up with this lady and i know she would never do that . . . she is very credible.

Mother of teenagers Says: I agree with Becky!!

Videographer

"It was a very violent scene. You could tell there was a lot that happened in there."—Detective Tim Helldorfer

"When your life is in disorder, and your home is in disorder, your mind is in disorder."—Juror

The eerily silent video walk-through of the New Haven murder scene was visually and emotionally powerful. About five hours after the first responders arrived the morning of June 5, and after eventually securing a consent to search from Noura, Tim Helldorfer, an experienced homicide detective of eleven and a half years, made the unusual decision to videotape the crime scene rather than submit the standard written account.

"After I did my walk-through," he said in an interview, "there was just no way I could describe it in writing. It was just absolutely too much stuff. There was no way. And when we describe a scene we start from the outside. We describe the layout of the house. In the front door and every room. I couldn't do it. I'd still be writing five years later."

It was almost four years later on day nine of the trial that he showed the jurors his original videotape. By then a criminal investigator for the district attorney, Helldorfer calmly and assuredly delivered his testimony. Having worked with television programs like *The First 48* (he is a perfect type-cast detective with his mustache and sturdy, compact frame), he strikes a chord as an experienced officer albeit one who can still be surprised.

The lights were dimmed in the packed and hushed courtroom. Initially Helldorfer narrated the tape but soon stopped, letting the video, with no accompanying audio tell the story. Complete silence fell over the room. The camera moved throughout Jennifer and Noura's home where many areas showed evidence markers already in place. Most shocking were the images of Jennifer's body still in her bedroom. Despite it being morning when the video was shot, its uneven lighting cast a menacing spell over the hallway and bedroom.

The sometimes shaky footage of the hand-held camera, along with its documentary style, recalled the well-known 1999 movie, *The Blair Witch Project.* At times, Jennifer's family and friends covered their eyes. Many cried. Her brother, Eric, with his head in his hands, sobbed, unprepared for the fresh grief that was unleashed. Noura viewed the video with her by-then typical enigmatic countenance.

Nick Kenney's blog for WMC-TV in Memphis chronicled Helldorfer's video tour, noting that it "show[ed] the entire bedroom in graphic detail":

> Starts at the front door from the outside looking in. Moves inside. To the right is the kitchen. Beyond the kitchen door is where the garage is. The door with the hole in it. The video shows the kitchen, the sink, the knife

> holder. Moves to the garage/kitchen door. The middle pane is broken in a perfect circle . . . There are storage shelves all over the garage. The garage is full of storage bins full of stuff. Stuff everywhere. . . . Back into the kitchen. Back into the foyer. Pans over the dining and living area. The sunroom in the background. The hallway. The common bathroom. The sink had water, [Helldorfer] says. . . . Noura's room. Can't see much the light is out. Jennifer's room. The bed is covered in blood. Jennifer's body is still there. Tight shot on the blood spatter on the pillow and the pool of blood on the bed. Tight shot of Jennifer's body laying on the floor. The video is graphic. Tight shot on the stab wounds. Very graphic. Video shows her whole body. Tight shot of the light switch covered in blood. The video tour continues. The floor of the master bedroom. A bloody print on the hardwood floor not far from Jennifer's body. Looks like a shoeprint. Back down the hallway with blood trail and evidence markers.

When the lights came up in the courtroom, the jurors appeared transformed. They gazed at Noura in a speculative manner. The once neutral, passive expressions of some were now intense and engaged. A female, African American juror in the first row gave Noura a penetrating and severe look.

"I think it was the best thing I did out there," Helldorfer said of the videotape. "It was my biggest mistake, but it was the best thing I did." The mistake, pounced upon by the defense team and many trial observers, was overlooking a shot of the wet shower. He testified to the hall shower being wet and some water in the bathroom sink but could not provide visual evidence that might have pointed to a sign a suspect was covering his or her tracks. "There's no doubt someone had taken a shower. You know how water beads up when it's drying? That's how it was," he said.

It was the first time he had ever videotaped a crime scene and "it showed," he said. "I should have filmed the outside of the house instead of starting at the front door. Should have shown the whole outer area. And I should have gone slower than I did. I just went too fast. And then the thing I really regret is not doing the bathroom. We had a photograph of the sink, but it doesn't adequately show it. . . . I had looked at the tub, and I had gone in with the camera, but it just didn't dawn on me. I was focusing on *the stuff.* I didn't focus, think, about the bath."

The stuff that caught his attention was everywhere. "I've seen houses with a lot of stuff," he said, "but never stuff never opened, never used. Still in wrappers, still in hanging clothes bags. I've never seen a house like that. [Jennnifer] had a shopper problem. Most of it was unopened."

Posts in *The Commercial Appeal* following the videotape were incredulous at the clutter and chaos of the home.

> **?8&^^%** Says: My goodness she had so much stuff in her shower/tub! At first I thought someone had ransacked her bathroom but

then i saw all the stuff hanging in there goodness.

Anon Says: It is obvious that both Jennifer and Noura used the hall bath to shower/bathe due to the clothing hanging on the shower curtain rod in the master bathroom. No way they could use that tub/shower!

NoRealProof Says: You think the bathroom is bad you should see the garage. You should see receipts where Jennifer bought 115 of 1 item.

"When we got there we were told she was stabbed ten or twelve times," Helldorfer said. "When I went back there I said, 'No, it was a whole lot more than that.' We classify that a rage killing. And a rage killing is done by someone who loves or hates somebody very close to them."

He noted that all the exterior doors to the house were secure. And to him, the round hole in the kitchen door to the garage looked staged. The door had three horizontal panes of glass, and the middle pane had a near-perfect round hole in it. "I've seen break-ins before. And it was obviously a staged break-in." It would take someone with knowledge of the house to be aware of the hinge lock visible only on the kitchen side of the door.

"Why would you break in through a window up high and reach up and through—which you could not do—to reach the door knob? You'd have to have an arm about five feet long to be able to do it. The only reason to break in up there was to unlock the latch (a sort of hidden hinge lock) that you can't see from the outside. You had to know it was there. There was no way you could see it. So where it was broken you could reach in, and the door opened right up. But if you didn't know it was there you couldn't do it. You wouldn't do it."

The unusual location of broken glass was Helldorfer's second red flag that morning. The first was Noura's reluctance to sign a consent to search. (Helldorfer arrived at 6:45 a.m., but it wasn't until 7:53 a.m. that Noura signed the consent.) A consent to search is faster than getting a search warrant—that would have been his next move—though it would have cost valuable time—another two or three hours. "The first thing I did [upon arriving at the scene] was shut everything down. Stopped everything because I wanted a search warrant or a consent to search. Noura refused to give us one and I knew then that she did it."

"I never, never had a family member refuse to give a consent to search. 'It's whatever you want, do it. I'll sign anything, whatever it takes.' She wouldn't do it. It took a family friend who happened to be an attorney to take her aside and explain to her what was going on. Red flag, big time. That's never happened before."

Crime Scene Officer David Payment spent two and a half days on the witness stand describing how possible evidence was recorded and collected. The blood-soaked bedding from the master bedroom—bed skirt to comforter, mattress pad to pillowcases—was entered into evidence.

Officer Payment also testified to finding blood, among other places, on the bedroom walls, closet doors, and the light switch on the bedroom wall. Payment used a measuring tape to estimate blood splatter as high as six feet on the closet doors. Blood also reached the light on the ceiling fan. Even given that, the blood splatter expert used by Memphis investigators, Forensic Serologist T. Paulette Sutton, did not come to the Jackson home the morning Jennifer was discovered.

The bloody trail from master bedroom continued all the way out to the front porch. Blood samples were taken from the hallway near the front door, the entry hall, the entryway mat, the front porch, and even from the front door itself just above the brass kick plate. These samples and most others taken throughout the house were positive for Jennifer's blood and DNA. Noura's blood, or her DNA of any kind, was absent from the crime scene.

Fingerprints proved as elusive as DNA results in the hunt for physical evidence. Experts compared known prints, a print deliberately taken, with latent prints, those inadvertently left on an object. Don Carpenter, a fingerprint expert for the prosecution, explained that individuals don't actually "leave" fingerprints. Instead a person leaves "ridge detail." Unknown prints were collected at the crime scene and compared with those that are known. Known prints are collected in a number of ways. Some people, like neighbors and friends, volunteer their prints; some are taken from employment records; and some from prior-arrest databases.

Carpenter processed a number of items for prints—including the wicker basket—but most yielded no results. Two drinking glasses on the kitchen counter, however, had ridge detail. At the time of the original investigation, these latent prints could not be matched. That changed just prior to the trial when Carpenter ran the prints again, and suddenly Kaole Madison was identified. In the intervening years, Kaole was convicted of a DUI offense, and his prints were in the system. This revelation came at the end of day seven, an intense day of testimony that included the medical examiner, and it seemed like a bombshell. It was the first time during the trial Kaole's name was mentioned. The very next day he found himself on the witness stand explaining why his prints were in the Jackson's kitchen, and his answer could not have been more ordinary. He'd had a drink of water before he and Noura left her house Saturday night, June 4.

Martin Milner, an expert in print identification, said Jennifer's prints, taken at the medical examiner's office, were not very clear, making it difficult for him to positively eliminate her from the Trojan condom wrapper found in her bedroom, though he could exclude Noura. The condom wrapper found on the floor near Jennifer's bedside table was never processed for DNA which was an omission defense attorney Corder mentioned a number of times.

On her cross-examination of Crime Scene Officer Payment—a tedious, grueling exercise that lasted one full day and part of another—she questioned the decision to send the wrapper away for fingerprint analysis rather than

DNA. The more she probed Payment about the mystery condom wrapper and its proximity to Jennifer's body, the more incredulous Corder's tone became. "You found a condom wrapper next to a naked, murdered woman. Wouldn't you want to check the bedside table for condoms?" she asked. "Did it occur to you that it might have been a sexual attack?" she continued. Neither the bedside table nor the trash can in the bedroom were inventoried.

"Noura's prints," Milner said, "were in rough shape for someone her age." He found their quality peculiar and surmised they looked more like prints belonging to a much older adult. Or perhaps someone who might have worked in construction. (WMC-TV reporter Nick Kenney blogged that at this testimony, "Noura appears surprised . . . and raised her eyebrows as if shocked or caught off guard.")

Milner considered known prints from Jennifer, Noura, Rachael Cocke, Kaole Madison, Mark Irvin, and Andrew Hammack. In the end the only latent print matched with a known print was that of Kaole Madison.

If DNA and fingerprints were dead ends, homicide detectives believed Noura's behavior quickly was helping build a case against her. Noura's incessant partying and all the different stories about the cut on her hand kept them focused on her. "We interviewed the kids. Because she wasn't arrested right away. And we interviewed people that she interacted with after the killing. And her behavior, and the way she acted. So we weren't following her or anything like that, but we followed where she went. We were hoping she would tell someone. That's what we wanted. We were hoping she'd say something to somebody. We had enough to arrest her right away, but there was no reason to do it," Helldorfer said. "She wasn't going anywhere; she wasn't a flight risk."

Requesting Noura and Jennifer's cell phone records on June 6, 2005, was one of their first tasks. These records do not contain any content of the calls or text messages but merely document the time of outgoing and incoming calls and texts. "Because we felt she was obviously involved we had to get on it. Cell phone records only remain for so long, and then they get rid of them. They destroy them," Helldorfer said. "We had to wait for all the cell phone records to come in. And then when you get them—keep in mind these are on the kids—the cell phone records you get at home as opposed to the ones we get when we subpoena are totally different. It is very confusing to look at and read. It takes a lot of time. And then we try to chart them and have a little graph going. This is to whom; this is so and so. It takes a long time to figure those out, and it takes weeks and weeks to get them back."

Noura's cell phone records the night of June 4 raised suspicion. Her almost constant cell phone use stopped between 1:00 a.m. and 3:00 a.m. with the exception of an incoming text message to her at 2:11 a.m. Helldorfer emphasized this in his *48 Hours* interview with Richard Schlesinger: "That cell phone was nonstop except for a limited time frame, which we feel was when the murder took place."

So detectives went about building a matricide case based on almost entirely circumstantial evidence. "There was no one thing that said 'she did it' because of this or this or this. You look at everything. It just kept adding up and adding up. It never pointed to anybody else. We looked at other people. It didn't go anywhere. It always kept coming back to her. . . . The worst thing from my point of view as an investigator is for an innocent person to spend a day in jail. To this I have never had a doubt about Noura. Never."

Though he felt confident early on about Noura's involvement, Helldorfer still puzzles over whether Jennifer was asleep and surprised by her daughter or if there was an argument between the two. "I am still to this day not sure. I kinda think there was an argument before she went to bed. Noura went and got a knife, walked down the hall, and then attacked her while she was sleeping. There's no doubt in my mind she was reclined in the bed when she was first hit. Whether she was awake or not I don't know. I think she was asleep. I can't . . . there's no way for me to know that."

Once the attack began, Jennifer's efforts were limited to self-defense. "There was a struggle, but it was all one sided because she was totally defenseless. She was trying to block the blows. To move and get away."

Exhibit Man

"If there was testimony that got real heavy—pictures of that woman lying there—when we would leave going down the hall, someone usually would have tears in their eyes. Someone would usually have like a small breakdown."—Juror

"Exhibit Man is asking again. He's given the appropriate exhibit number and seems satisfied until the next exhibit question arises." Commercial Appeal *Trial Blog*

The unique vantage of a jury—that isolated, impartial, outside audience—inevitably fascinates anyone who has closely followed a trial. Their perspective is the most coveted when a verdict is reached. The eight women and four men charged with deciding Noura's fate were drawn from diverse educational, economic, and racial backgrounds. They were forbidden from discussing Noura's case among themselves until deliberations began or with anyone else during the fourteen days they were sequestered.

Jury selection began the morning of February 9, 2009. Trial Judge Christopher Craft anticipated a lengthy trial and decided on three alternates instead of the usual two.

To help keep all jurors engaged, no one on the jury would know his or her status as an alternate until moments before deliberations began. At that point a random process would eliminate the alternates. Craft's decision proved prescient. Only three days into the trial the jury was down by two. One juror's husband had a heart attack, and another juror suffered an extreme migraine. These circumstances prompted Craft to write in email on February 13, 2009: "I have only lost 2 jurors twice since 1994. Never have I lost 3. However, today is Friday the 13th, a side-view mirror fell off the jury bus and shattered onto the expressway this morning, a black cat showed up in the crime scene photographs, a plane went down and two satellites crashed into each other. We'll just have to see if we can get through the day."

From an initial pool of sixty people, what came to be the final fifteen gradually took shape. Prospective jurors knew from the outset that they would be sequestered. Craft believed media coverage might affect their deliberations. Before the selection process even started Monday morning, the defense called Craft's attention to reporter Lawrence Buser's *Commercial Appeal* article, "Building a Case for Matricide," in Sunday's (February 8, 2009) paper as potentially tainting a jury. The defense said they found some of the posted online comments accompanying the story "quite disturbing."

> **CarterHaugh**: I hereby nominate Noura to be the official poster child for the pro-choice movement. Geesh, talk about your daughter from HELL!

> **fishnlawyr:** That little precious, prestigious, private school drop-out had 1.4 million reasons to do her mother. That can certainly buy her at least a week's supply of crystal meth. Save your sobbing hankys for someone more deserving.

As the jury observed Noura and other witnesses, trial observers watched the jury. In Tennessee jurors are allowed to ask questions of witnesses making them slightly less inscrutable. Often the jurors' questions—reviewed by the judge and posed to the witness—offered a window into their thoughts.

One particular, seemingly compulsive juror asked an abundance of questions about specific exhibit numbers in a trial that included nearly 400 exhibits. *Commercial Appeal* blogger Clay Bailey dubbed him "Exhibit Man." And while his questions may have been tiresome, they also provided a welcome bit of humor. A juror interviewed said that when Exhibit Man "raised his hand, [the jurors] would exchange looks. Sometimes he asked questions that had just been answered!" she said. He surprised everyone one day when he asked a substantial question of Eric Sherwood. Sherwood testified about seeing condoms in Noura's bedroom. Bailey blogged, "Exhibit Man, the juror who usually wants to know the number of an exhibit, asks about the brand of condoms. Sherwood doesn't know about them other than it was a blue package."

Those following the *Commercial Appeal* blog were soon referencing Exhibit Man. Faithful blogger **Paducahdry** predicted Sherwood's slip on the stand—when he mentioned Charter Lakeside Hospital by name—would prove significant for the jury:

> **Paducahdry** Says: You can be sure someone from the jury picked up on it and it will be a point of discussion during deliberations.
>
> **sam** Says: yes i'm sure one of the jurors did, i'm sure the exhibit man picked up on it lol!

Conversely, there was another juror who asked a lot of pertinent questions called "Question Man." The two jurors were confused by some bloggers.

> **JCC** Says: Was the juror that was excused "Exhibit Man?"

In the end, Exhibit Man was one of the two holdouts against first degree, and no one will ever know how Question Man might have impacted the verdict. Ironically, he was chosen as the alternate juror. His numerous questions—usually about the lack of physical evidence—suggested that he was sympathetic toward the defense arguments. The juror interviewed agreed. She felt early on that based on his questions he was not inclined toward a guilty verdict. "I know the other side—defense—must have been very disappointed when he was dismissed," she said.

Over the course of those days jury members also heard various opinions about Noura's childhood, personality, and what might have happened that June morning. After the trial, one juror spoke at length about her insights and perceptions. She personally took over ninety pages of notes during the trial, but jury instructions prior to deliberations included the admonition that notes were for private use only "as an aid to individual memory."

Once the case was decided she said the jury was "warned up and down not to speak to anyone" by "everyone involved." They were told that Noura's lawyers would use anything they could "to discredit the jury and get Noura a new trial." She along with the other jurors decided not to appear on *48 Hours*. "We were all scared to death of helping Noura." She would not say who cautioned them against speaking, but it seems unlikely it would have been anyone from the defense team.

"I felt like the earth had been pulled out from under me," she said, once she realized she was an official member of the jury. And when it was over she hoped "it would go away and I could scrub it from my memory." A task that proved difficult if not impossible as she found the "visual of the murder" to be overwhelming with a killer who did "mean and unthinkable things."

Three and a half years had passed between the date of her arrest, September 29, 2005, and jury selection. During that time Noura had been in jail and largely out of the public eye. Over those years she made numerous court appearances, but with time media attention diminished.

Unless something exceptional happened, her court dates generally went unreported. She was swept into the groaning gears of the court process.

The attention and visits she received from her peers while she was in jail likewise dwindled. At first there were a lot of visits from friends and Perry. But his visits stopped, and others soon trailed off. These were the same kids who were partying with Noura and even spending the night with her in the aftermath. Noura keenly felt everyone had turned on her, from her family to her former East Memphis crowd. The so-called friends were no more than that. A hard and bitter reality. All of which made a letter Noura received in jail especially surprising. Though Kirby and Noura had perhaps more disagreements with each other than most of the group, Kirby wrote her a note after her arrest saying that "Regardless of the situation, [she] loved her as a friend and was thinking of [her]."

Cut off from the maternal relatives who actively sought her conviction and sued her, and with her father's relatives either living in Lebanon or uninvolved with her fate, Noura depended on a few close friends who continued to stand by her. Noura's core supporters—Bill Shelton, Jennifer's former boyfriend; Ansley Larsson, the mother of Noura's past boyfriend; Dana Fredrick, the mother of Noura's friends; Gloria Hodge, her father's friend; and Renae McMillan, formerly married to Noura's uncle Eric—remained steadfast.

Bill Shelton never missed a court date. Even though she hadn't been a part of his life for years, when Shelton read about Noura's arrest in the paper he immediately went to see her, and his support did not waver. Noura was arrested on a Thursday, and he saw her the following Sunday.

He rode down the elevator with a homicide detective and told the officer, “I can’t believe she did it.”

The officer replied, “You shouldn’t put yourself out there. Be supportive but she’s guilty.”

Shelton said that from the first moments of her arrest there was a concerted campaign against Noura. When some of her family members found out about his friendship with Noura and that he had visited with her at the jail, they called him and asked him not to support her. “They lost the right to be called family quite a while ago,” he said. Faced with the daunting task of cleaning out Jennifer’s home, Grace and Cindy asked Shelton to care for Noura’s personal possessions. “We had somehow learned that Bill Shelton was on Noura’s side,” Grace said, “and since no family members were on her side, we tried to find the best person to guard Noura’s personal effects. Noura was incarcerated, so she couldn’t come to the house to say what she wanted.”

According to Noura’s confidants, she speaks frequently about her mom and often cries. She told Richard Schlesinger on *48 Hours Mystery* that her grief process was disturbed: “My grief was interrupted,” she said, “because when you get arrested and you have your back up against the wall and you’re constantly having, y’know, to explain, ‘I didn’t do this, I didn’t do this.’ You don’t have time to grieve. You have to defend yourself.”

She adamantly maintains her innocence and struggles even more with dates like her mother’s birthday, Mother’s Day, and the anniversary of Jennifer’s death. Noura told Schlesinger, “In the morning when I wake up in a cell . . . and you have to remind yourself why you’re here . . . my mother’s dead. You can’t help but relive it every morning you wake up.”

It is as Christina Wieland describes in her book, *The Undead Mother*, that far from dispatching someone from your life, murder makes the victim as close as the killer's own shadow. The haunting presence is at times more vivid than others, but it is always a companion. "Murder can never be the basis for separation," Wieland writes. "Far from resulting in separation from the object, it leads instead on the contrary, to the perpetual presence of a persecutory object and to melancholia."[14]

For the first year of her incarceration Noura appeared before Criminal Court Judge Arthur Bennett. When Bennett retired in September 2006, Noura's case was transferred to Judge Christopher Craft. Bennett's courtroom method was a strong contrast to Craft's. Bennett's bailiffs often questioned visiting members of the public as to whose case they were observing. Whenever Noura heard her name mentioned she turned around inquisitively.

In Bennett's court, Noura and all the female inmates with motions and hearings sat together on a bench. They sometimes talked, even joked, among themselves. Groups of women in the blazing orange outfits. And given Memphis's demographics, Noura fairly often was the only Caucasian female inmate. The relaxed atmosphere matched a frequently off-task schedule with the end result being numerous breaks and long waits. An exercise in endurance.

Only one inmate appeared at a time—usually cuffed to the bench rail—before Craft, and he typically kept a

[14] Ibid, 117.

precise schedule. Judge Craft's round eyeglass frames gave him the bespectacled look of a wise owl. He was attentive and engaged and, for a criminal court judge, unruffled and pleasant. Yet if some courtroom protocol or ethic was breached, he could exhibit volcanic anger.

During this same time period over various pretrial motions and hearings—the defense, Valerie Corder and Arthur Quinn; and the prosecution, Amy Weirich, Steve Jones, and Alexia Fulgham—squared off. The defense team also procured the service of Clark Chapman, a private investigator, who assisted on many levels, especially in attempting to interview would-be trial witnesses. A tall man with a friendly, open demeanor, Chapman dispelled many of the private investigator clichés. His interest in people and complex relationships no doubt served him well in his work, as did his wide smile and relaxed manner. It was easy to appreciate his moniker, "Clark Kent." However, even with all that in his favor, there were some prosecution witnesses, among them Genevieve Dix, Eric Sherwood, and Noura's friend Kirby McDonald, who refused to talk with him. (Kirby talked with him early on, but on his later attempt, she said her parents advised her not to.)

No doubt Craft expected a fiery trial much like what he had sampled in preliminary motions. Female attorneys, both fierce and hard driving, led each team. Corder earned her reputation as a strong client advocate who would not back down, and Weirich was skilled, determined, and moving up in the criminal law world. Jokes about potential catfights made the rounds. The two attorneys sparred in a professional and frequently testy manner. In January of 2011 Weirich was named Shelby County's first female district attorney.

Corder and Weirich were perfectly balanced by their co-counsels, Art Quinn and Steve Jones. A *Commercial Appeal* photograph shows the four attorneys facing Judge Craft in one of their frequent bench conferences. Corder and Weirich are standing side by side—each woman in a gray suit, hair of similar length and color—and from behind they are bookends. Quinn stands to Corder's left, and Jones to Weirich's right. Calm and steady, Quinn and Jones tempered their co-counsel's combative nature. Their approach was no less effective. Quinn especially was adept at cross-examinations of the teenagers and Jennifer's siblings. The even, persuasive tone of Jones' closing as he summarized the prosecution's case accomplished his purpose: "This case is about Jennifer Jackson. Her life and her death. It's about her life because she is the only one who stood in the way of the defendant and her life style of freedom to do whatever she wanted. . . . And it's about Jennifer's death because in these two weeks her killer gets held accountable."

Initially Noura was quite animated during her hearings. She almost reveled in the attention from reporters. During an early court appearance, she looked around, smiling, and asked brightly, "Where is Larry?" referring to *Commercial Appeal* reporter Lawrence Buser. As one year turned to two, she presented differently. She plainly struggled with her moods, increasingly was despondent, and appeared disinterested in anything happening around her. Her bulkier frame symptomatic of her deepening depression. Often she seemed in physical discomfort and motioned for a female bailiff. That usually ensured some sort of reprieve from the courtroom.

Noura was thin with heavily highlighted, professionally styled hair at the time of her arrest. So when jury selection commenced, reporters struggled for ways to describe her altered appearance. The *Commercial Appeal* blogger settled on a "fuller face." "Unlike previous pictures of the defendant she now has dark hair instead of the blonde look that she had in previous pictures. Her face also looks fuller than expected."

With the weight gain, dark clothes and hair, Noura was a somber, almost matronly version of her former self. Television reporter Kontji Anthony remarked on how changed she was—the way she sat hunched over in her chair—and questioned why no one was there to support Noura the day of jury selection. In her evening report Anthony returned to those themes, "It was clear Monday," she said, "she had no family anywhere nearby. The only people in or outside the courtroom were court staffers, potential jurors, a national TV show, and a book author. Jackson wore a dark suit and sat slumped in her seat whispering with her attorneys." Cameras were not allowed inside that day, but Anthony predicted that "In the chambers of Criminal Court Judge Chris Craft an explosive trial was about to unfold."

Anthony keyed in on Noura's stark loneliness and alienation from family. That fact soon was illustrated. With sixty potential jurors crammed in the courtroom, Craft asked Noura to stand and face them; to make sure no one was acquainted with her. A more awkward scenario hardly could be imagined. Noura tried a brief smile as she looked around the room. Without her attorneys or even court staffers beside her, she faced the room in solitude, the agonizing moment awash in pain.

No one seemed certain where the outfit Noura was wearing at the time of her arrest wound up, or, for that matter, what happened to her remaining clothes at New Haven. Therefore, most of Noura's trial outfits were courtesy of her lawyer. Corder gave her credit card to a young, female assistant and asked her to go shopping. After selecting a number of items—and after a consult with Noura for sizes and ideas—Noura mentioned "wife beaters" which was deemed inappropriate—she traveled with the clothing selections to Jail East.

Corder's assistant was surprised that Noura had to try the clothes on in a well-lit room behind glass. Wearing some sort of makeshift, jail undergarments. She expressed her embarrassment for Noura but said she seemed unfazed by it and apparently was growing accustomed to her loss of privacy.

No doubt Noura looked forward to dressing differently from the day-to-day jail garb. She experimented with her waist-length hair. Some days it would be down with loose curls; some days pulled back in a ponytail or worn straight. On at least two occasions it was pulled up in front with the ends curled. She wore makeup, and every now and then you were reminded of what an attractive young woman she was.

If the defense was going for a serious and respectable look for her, the unfortunate result was that Noura's personality was muted by the dark colors or heavy textures.

And when she wore patterned or brightly colored clothes, the outfits were a little too jolting. Throughout the course of the trial, achieving a tasteful, even wardrobe for Noura proved difficult.

For jury selection, she chose a cowl-neck light yellow sweater with a black jacket. She looked tense and uncomfortable in the weighty garments. Afterward she alternated a few outfits. The brown jacket and cream shirt she selected for the first day of trial testimony was an improvement as well as her more relaxed expression. Whether she wore slacks, a skirt, or dress, there was usually some sort of layer. The sweaters or jackets, along with her slumped posture, had her looking older and graver than her years. The blouses offered relief. They varied from white to sea foam to pastels. One day she appeared in an incongruous green and black patterned peasant top. Almost always the solid colored blouses suited her best.

The day of closing arguments she surprised in a boldly patterned top, with bright blue flowers and a navy background. When the verdict came in she was wearing a blue, flowered dress and navy sweater she burrowed into.

In a manner, the dark clothes exaggerated her placid mood, but sometimes a spirited Noura would show up. Like the day Grace France testified. Throughout the trial, her attorneys warned Noura not to so much as turn around to see those seated behind the defense or prosecution tables. She had adhered to this advice, so it was a surprise when she strongly reacted to Grace. Her aunt Grace's testimony proved that even if she purposely was estranged from her mother's family, they could still infuriate her. Grace provoked an outburst from Noura—the only one of the trial—though her attorney quickly stifled it.

For Grace, like her sister Cindy, the witness chair was a land mine. The sisters shed tears and responded—sometimes tersely—to defense attorney Quinn's probing questions. Grace said she kept asking Noura about the cut on her hand and said she asked her niece to "Just tell us the truth." To which Noura mouthed angrily "I am telling the truth." In a split second Corder had her hand clamped securely over Noura's mouth.

Noura also had broken from her usual trance-like state when her aunt Cindy testified the day before Grace. Unlike the visible anger she directed at Grace, Noura cried and appeared genuinely upset by Cindy's characterization of the Memorial Day weekend at her Florida home, as well as other events both before and after the murder. Most likely because she was more involved in her niece's life, Cindy's appearance aroused a softer, sadder response from her niece. In the past, Noura had visited Cindy's home with her friends during spring breaks. The summer of 2004 Clark Schifani and Brooke Thompson had vacationed with the Noura and Jennifer in Florida.

Noura had an even tighter bond with Eric. Eric lived at times with Jennifer and Noura, the three forming a nuclear family of sorts. Eric's deep regard for his sister was evident by his emotional volatility during the trial. During a trip to Jennifer's house after her death Eric found his sister's wallet. It was in an uncovered plastic bin in the sunroom near a door leading to the backyard. Inside he found her bank card, Social Security card, company card, Triple AAA motor club card, and others. The discovery prompted him to call homicide detectives.

When Eric testified that Noura asked her mother about her life insurance policy, Noura was incredulous, later telling Richard Schlesinger, "How convenient for me to be asking about life insurance a week before my mother's murder. I don't know."

"Are you calling your uncle a liar?" he asked.

"Yes. And that's hard to do because," she said with a pause. "Umm, I love him."

Grace, Cindy, Eric, and other relatives attended almost all pretrial motions and hearings, sitting behind the prosecution table. For Grace and Cindy that meant frequent trips from their respective home in Atlanta, Georgia, and Winter Park, Florida. They were often huddled with the prosecution team in the hallway. There was no mistaking their allegiance. Should Noura be found guilty, Jennifer's estate would be split among her siblings. On October 18, 2005, the fair-market value of Jennifer's estate was recorded as follows:

Life Insurance Payable to Estate, Cash,	
Marketable Securities	$1,250,000
Automobiles	
and Other Personal Property	$50,000
Real Estate	$171,800
Total	$1,426, 800
Less:	
Debts Secured by Real Estate	$135,000

The Jackson siblings also filed a wrongful death civil suit against Noura, seeking $14 million in compensatory and punitive charges. The complaint was filed May 26,

2006, almost three years before the February 2009 trial, on behalf of "Frank M. Eidson [Cindy Eidson's husband] and Jon W. Smith, personal representative of the estate of Jennifer S. Jackson, deceased." The complaint alleges the "Defendant intentionally killed her mother in a horrible and gruesome manner, by stabbing her repeatedly" and that the "Defendant's conduct makes her liable to plaintiffs for punitive damages."

Noura's criminal attorneys were not representing her in this civil matter, so Noura composed a formal answer to the wrongful death complaint. Whether or not she had assistance from other parties is unknown. She responded that "The Complaint is brought for the sole purpose of harassment, to cause unnecessary delay, to needlessly increase the cost of litigation, and is not warranted by existing law. . . . The Complaint is brought out of greed and avarice, and is without foundation in fact or law, but is merely an attempt by the Defendants to appropriate Plaintiff's inheritance from her mother to themselves by making claims, known to be false and fraudulent, against Defendant, using Defendant's inheritance from her mother to finance their nefarious endeavor."

Judge Bailey, on November 15, 2006, ordered a stay of all discovery and proceedings until "a final disposition of all criminal charges against the defendant."

The issue fired up again in May of 2007 when Frank Eidson and Jon Smith filed a motion to amend their wrongful death complaint. Noura believed a hearing on the motion had been scheduled without her notification. Using 6201 Haley Road (Jail East) as her return address, Noura inquired about a potential hearing in a handwritten letter to Circuit Court Judge D'Army Bailey. Noura's May

16, 2007, letter is composed in beautiful cursive similar to her mother's handwriting:

> *Judge D'Army Bailey,*
>
> *My name is Noura Jackson. My docket # is CT-002756-06. A friend of mine told me he heard I have a hearing coming up in your courtroom. I thought I would be notified of any hearings. I have not been notified. As an inmate, Jail East would have had me sign for any legal notices from a court or a law firm. I have received no legal notices and have not signed any legal notices.*
>
> *I am requesting that you let me complete my first degree murder case before any steps are taken in the wrongful death case. My mother is the victim in both cases. As a 20 year old inmate in a first degree murder case with no bond and no resources, at this time I am unable to identify and research wrongful death attorneys, contact them, interview them, make a selection, and adequately assist that attorney in the preparation of my defense. I would be unable to attend hearings or the trial. I assure you, the wrongful death case will have my full attention once I have completed the first degree murder case.*
>
> *Thank you for your consideration.*

Sincerely,

Noura Jackson

When defense counsel Art Quinn questioned Grace about the civil suit, she said, "I don't need the money. I want my sister." She said the evidence against Noura was mounting, and the family was informed they had only one year to file a civil suit. Grace told Quinn that the family had not liked Nazmi, and though she was not terribly close to Noura, she loved her. "I loved Noura. I didn't want it to be Noura. I've lost a sister and a niece. For one of our own family to murder another is terrible. We didn't want it to be Noura."

According to Judge Craft, before the trial began Jennifer's sisters had a representative request that cameras not show them. They were angry that cameras were allowed into the courtroom at all. Craft, a firm believer in an open courtroom and as much transparency as possible, denied the request. Craft believed Noura's aunts didn't want their life style inconvenienced by their niece.

That perhaps explains how the two decided to rent an apartment for a troubled, eighteen-year-old girl, yet to complete high school to live in alone. After her release from Charter Lakeside Hospital toward the end of June 2005, Noura needed a place to live. Cindy and Grace suggested Noura find a one-bedroom apartment in the $500 to $600 month range. Noura rejected that idea, telling her aunts "I'm used to living in a nice house. Have you seen what a $500 or $600 apartment looks like?" They eventually found a nicer, two-bedroom apartment (higher rent of course), in a Bartlett apartment complex where her uncle Eric lived and worked doing building maintenance for the complex. Noura lived there about one month until frequent parties resulted in her eviction.

At the time Noura was apartment hunting, Jennifer's estate was unresolved, so Grace, Cindy, and her husband, Frank Eidsen, were paying Noura's expenses. Tensions escalated as Noura insisted on a nicer apartment and more spending money. Many of their conversations with Noura during that time were long distance and involved the unsavory topic of money. These phone calls probably introduced conflicting feelings. Should I take care of my sister's daughter or cast aside her killer?

"If they feel guilty about Noura Jackson, they'll buy a mink coat. Plan a trip. They don't want to talk about the case because they do feel guilty," Craft surmised. The day after Noura's conviction, her aunts hosted a "celebration lunch." Not fully comprehending the various allegiances, Linda Finlay mistakenly invited Dana Fredrick. The lunch was another disturbing development for Dana following on the heels of the verdict.

Second Degree

"I can be here two weeks. If you want to be in this room two weeks, I'm your man."— Juror during jury deliberations

Noura's rejection by Jennifer's family factored into how the juror interviewed assessed her childhood. "This girl had a horrible childhood," she said. "Everyone hated her father. Her father was dead. Her father was cut out of her life. By his choice or by the family's choice. So Noura had no one on her side. She felt like that. So therefore she had no one to impress. She didn't have her father's people. Her mother's people didn't like her father. So she's a man without a country. Therefore there wasn't anyone she had to hold up to in her eyes. She didn't have to do anything for anybody. The only people that she had were the people her own age. And by golly she was going to do what it took to be in that group. They were the important people. They were her life."

She noted also that Noura had no place to keep order. "My mom always said it was important to have your bedroom and your things in order for the next morning so that the day can be in order. When you live in a home like that, it's got to mess you up."

Interestingly the jury did not consider Jennifer's financial success—and Noura's desire for her father's money—of any real importance despite the prosecution's suggestion of it as a motive. And as far as the Jackson siblings inheriting Jennifer's estate, the juror agreed that seemed reasonable: "People felt in there [the jury deliberations] that if she had murdered her mother, that they should get the estate. That she shouldn't get it. It was a very sensible decision. They were all sensible about that part.

"I don't believe that really entered into it with any of us," she said. "People understood that she had money. And that it went wrong. And I think that as a general group we understood that it can happen whether you have money or not.

"We understood that they did have some money at some points. And that they didn't do so well at other points. We just never thought about the money part of it."

If the jury didn't, other people certainly did. The prosecution made much of Noura and Jennifer's arguments over money, and Jennifer's family asserted that her healthy finances served as a "death warrant." According to the impassioned victim impact statement, "[Jennifer] provided for herself from the age of 17. She brought her half-brother to live with her and Noura, making sure he finished high school and got a good start in life. She tried to do the same for Noura by providing love, attention, encouragement, the best private schools and every advantage in life that she could, but Noura chose a life of drugs and partying. It is sickening to realize that Jennifer's efforts to provide financial security for she (sic) and Noura may actually have sealed her own death warrant."

While watching Noura closely those fourteen days, the female juror interviewed came to believe her flat expression was simply "who Noura was. I believe that whatever happened to her in her childhood just disconnected her somehow. Emotionally. I think she was totally disconnected from people in a way. Disconnected from the family I think through her own choice. She didn't look . . . Noura just didn't look quite right sitting there to me. She just looked like she had major mental issues to me."

When the verdict was read she found Noura consistently expressionless, "I don't think she was surprised at all because there was absolutely *no* surprise on her face at all. None. She knew."

Outside the eyes of trial observers, almost daily breakdowns occurred among jurors. Someone would be in tears. When not in the courtroom the jury occupied two rooms, one with windows, one without. One day a young, male juror went into the vacant room, put his head down on the table, and sobbed. The other jury members missed him and found him there. "I didn't want it to be her. I didn't want it to be her," he said to no one but himself. When they tried to comfort him, he cried, "This is so horrible! This is so horrible!"

This breakdown occurred after day ten's testimony that cinched the prosecution's case as far as the jury was concerned—"When it all started coming together." A Walgreens surveillance videotape captured Noura at

4:14 a.m. purchasing New-Skin, a liquid bandage, tape, hydrogen peroxide, and other wound care items. Those items were recovered in Noura's Jeep—still in a Walgreens bag—with some loose change. Sergeant W. D. Merritt took forty dollars cash to Walgreens, bought the exact five items, and received the same change.

"I'm going to tell you what, if you ever commit a crime, you don't want W.D. Merritt on your trail. He's so good," Helldorfer said. "He single handedly went out to get the video of the guy at Walgreens which actually showed him getting her a towel to wipe her hand."

Merritt told Schlesinger on *48 Hours*, "I asked the manager if we could review her video surveillance system. Low and behold, here comes Noura walking into Walgreens." The visual of the clerk handing her paper towels that she then pressed to her hand—"to dab her bleeding wound," Detective Justice said—was difficult for the defense to banish.

"That's when Noura's story started falling to the wayside," the juror said. "She just walks right in, picks up what she needs, goes up there, puts it down. She asks him for a paper towel, and he rolls out a big bunch of paper towels, cuts it off, hands it to her. She wraps it up in her hand and walks right out the door. She acted just normal." Keith McDonald, the Walgreens night clerk, said he remembered Noura "because [a paper towel] was not a normal request."

At the outset of the trial the juror believed all members felt sympathy for Noura. "I think even toward the end some of the women probably felt sympathy for her," she said. "I wish to God I could. I wish I felt sympathy for her because I feel really bad that I don't. But I think I don't because of the visual of the killing. I just . . . it was just such a horrible way to kill somebody. I just can't. I'm sorry."

On Saturday, February 21, 2009, at 8:30 a.m., Judge Craft released the alternate juror, Question Man, and deliberations began in earnest. Craft's parting instructions to the jury was both liberating and burdensome. "He told us to 'take as long as we needed; to try not and throw any chairs. 'Now,' he said, 'it is in your hands.'" The jury took the judge's reminder to heart, and for roughly nine and a half hours, dedicated themselves to working through the evidence and reaching a verdict. However, in the end it wasn't the issue of innocence or guilt that divided them. By midmorning they were in agreement about Noura's guilt.

"When the foreperson of the jury stood up and asked, 'We all agree she did it?' Everyone said yes," the juror revealed. They agreed also the murder was premeditated.

Then for eight hours deliberations stalled on a first- or second-degree verdict. Ten jurors were satisfied with first degree; two jurors, though they concurred that it was first-degree murder, rejected the idea of leaving the room with it. One of the holdouts was Exhibit Man "He was concerned about *everything*," the juror said. The other holdout was also a male juror. "He said they could give her the death penalty, and he wasn't going to go along. He said quite vocally, 'I can be here two weeks. If you want to be in this room two weeks, I'm your man.'" He did not believe in capital punishment.

The prosecution had said frequently in pretrial motions that Noura's was not a capital case. That information, however, somehow escaped the jury. Defense attorney Art Quinn said he appreciated the manner in which Judge Craft handled the jury instructions. "He told the jury not to be concerned about punishment," Quinn said. The jury did not know for certain that it was *not* a capital case. "That," he said, "might have worked in our favor."

Also, Noura's gender, age, and improbably, her drug use, helped her with some. "I didn't read that in the book," the juror emphasized, referring to what her own conscience was telling her. "[That] when we went in the room it said 'If she's young, if she's on drugs, you don't have to do murder one.' I didn't read that." She disagreed with the second degree verdict, noting that Noura would be about the same age as her mother upon her release. "Imagine how her family feels. Wouldn't it be better to know she would never be out? She might kill again."

The juror believed the murder was premeditated as defined in the jury instructions they received: "A premeditated act is one done after the exercise of reflection and judgment. Premeditation means that the intent to kill must have been formed prior to the act itself. It is not necessary that the purpose to kill preexist in the mind of the accused for any definite period of time."

More simply put, there must be *the period of time needed for reflection.* In this case, the time it took Noura to walk to the kitchen for a knife or knives and down the hall to her mother's bedroom.

"I think when she went in there she'd been mad all night; her world had been turned upside down," the juror explained. "She saw that unless something happened it was over for her. I think when she went in that room and she got her mother. She stabbed her mother."

The crime scene report acknowledged a possible shoe print on the upper-left corner of the bed. The juror thinks Noura put her foot on the bed, almost anchored herself, for the first, powerful stab that served to essentially immobilize her mother. Then she sat on the side of the bed (where part of the sheet was free of blood) and continued the assault.

"One foot on the bed—down real quick—pop pop pop. And then you notice there was no DNA on [Jennifer's] fingernails. Okay. If you're a mom, and it's your child, you're going to look up and you're going to be . . . to realize, 'Oh, my God.' And you're going to think, 'This can't be happening.' You're going to block but you're not going to hurt your child. You're just not going to do it. So she blocked and rolled. And that's where the [stab wounds] come up on the side. She didn't scratch. You just can't—in your heart—you just can't scratch your child. You can fight back by pushing your daughter off of you, but you're not going to scratch."

She speculated Noura's hand injury occurred when she positioned her mother's neck at an angle. "When she took her hand and pushed back [her mom's neck], and she started this [demonstrates knife's movement], that's how she got the cut on her hand, doing this across her mom's neck. Her hand got in the way. Somehow she put her hand up to push her mom's neck back and . . . that woman's neck had to have been pushed back. . . . She had to have lifted with one hand and was cutting with the other."

As certain as she was of Noura's murderous intent, the juror conceded there could also be another scenario. She had reared children and noted that girls, especially, "can be pistols." As time passed it became clear two jurors would not walk out with a first- degree verdict. "We didn't want a hung jury because of the money, the time. We didn't want that. So then somebody said, 'Well, what if she didn't mean to do it?'"

They constructed a second degree scenario built around a confrontation between mother and daughter. "And I said it could have been this way. And it could have. Because I'm a mom, and I really love my children, and here is how it could have come down in real life. Noura walks in the house. Jennifer is in the bed asleep. She sits up 'Noura, where have you been? You're late. And have you been seeing Perry?'

"'Mom, I don't want to talk about that right now. You know I love Perry. Yes, I saw him.'

"'Noura we've been over this. We're going to deal with it tomorrow and next week you're in boarding school. This is it, this is the last time. I'm going to bed and we'll talk about it tomorrow.'

"She rolls over. Noura, furious, walks to the kitchen, picks up a knife. She comes back. Just out of her mind. She'd been doing drugs; she hadn't had any sleep. Whacks her mom. I mean bam.

And that was second degree."

A Ride Downtown

"My role was to take Noura to the station to get a statement. Noura rode in the front seat of my unmarked police vehicle. We left about 8:15, and she was buckled in. She slept all the way to 201 Poplar. I had to wake her up when we got there." —Homicide Detective Connie Justice

Connie Justice also was summoned to 5001 New Haven early that Sunday morning. A homicide detective for eight years, Justice had a total of twenty-four years with the Memphis Police Department. She arrived about 7:40 a.m. and was assigned the task of getting a witness statement from Noura. By then Noura had talked with a number of officers—never quite giving the same story twice according to neighbor Sheila Cocke—and reluctantly signed a consent to search the house at 7:53 a.m.

At 8:17 a.m., Noura and Justice left New Haven for 201 Poplar. Justice was in her plain clothes, and Noura rode beside her in the front seat of the unmarked car. Noura was not handcuffed nor Mirandized. In fact, she couldn't have been more relaxed, sleeping all the way there.

In all Justice spent about four hours with Noura that morning at police headquarters. Most of that time Noura was upset about her new kitten at home. "She was manageable," Justice said, describing Noura's demeanor, "but overall she was ready to go. Bordering on kind of uncooperative. She seemed sort of put out with having to be there and was ready to go." At 10:53 a.m., Justice had Noura sign a consent to search her Jeep. Detective Tim Helldorfer, still at the scene, looked in the Jeep for blood or any type of evidence. He didn't see anything that prompted him to further investigate the vehicle at that time.

Meanwhile, Justice took a seven page, typewritten witness statement at her desk while Noura sat nearby. Justice typed her questions spontaneously and then typed Noura's responses. The conversation did not take place in an interrogation room, and the document was not a "suspect" statement. Noura's statement was taken only because she was the person who found her mother's body that morning.

Although she received additional phone calls off and on from investigators, as well as a visit from Justice and another female detective for more thorough photographs of her body, this was Noura's only official questioning by police. The day after the murder, her aunt Grace called her at the Menkel home where Noura was visiting to say she was going to police headquarters. Perhaps because she was the eldest, Grace was chosen by the family to be the contact person with the Memphis Police Department. Noura staunchly declined going with her, saying, "I'm not going back down there."

Noura's witness statement was almost the only time her voice was heard outside of a few times in the courtroom.

In pretrial motions there were technical matters that required her to take the witness stand: to try to prove her ownership of the Jeep Cherokee; to ensure that she understood the implications of setting a trial date and the possible sentencing lengths should she be convicted of first degree or second degree murder; to testify to her indigent status; and at her bond hearing. Her young and courteous voice always was surprising to hear, making it even more implausible to imagine her capable of such an atrocious crime.

Twenty-nine months had passed with Noura in jail before her February 5, 2008, bond hearing. Judge Craft asked her how he could be assured she would come to court if he granted bond. "The only important people left in my life live here. I have no one else," she said. Upon release, she would live with Bill Shelton and work on her GED as well as help her defense team prepare for trial. Valerie Corder pointed out that Noura knew she was under investigation between June and September 2005, and had made no effort to flee. The prosecution reacted strongly, citing the strength of their case and the fact that "Noura's aunts and other family members are against her release." Craft set a $500,000 bond, saying, "She's entitled to bond, but she's a big question mark. She may be a resentful, out-of-control teenager. I don't know." In the end no one so inclined had the available funds for her bond. Some said Corder's strategy was to keep Noura in jail and out of trouble until the trial began.

During the murder trial Noura took the stand to explain her relationship with her mother's friend, attorney Genevieve Dix, and their conversation at New Haven regarding the consent to search the Jackson home and their vehicles.

Her brief time on the witness stand excited a number of blog comments about Noura's accent. Strangers asked if she was Cajun; others wondered how long she had been in the jail.

She sounded quite different to people who knew her, and, admittedly, she had picked up a jailhouse accent. Three and half years of incarceration had altered not only her physical appearance, but also her speech.

> **caitlin** Says: her old voice creeps out for a second . . . it was just for a second but she sounded like she used to. did anyone notice that? my very first thought too i cant believe it is possible for her voice to have changed that much.

> **get real** Says: i knew noura . . . and whoaaa . . . she did NOT TALK LIKE THAT its probably bc she sounds like the people shes in jail with . . . bahhahahah

The random nature of Detective Justice's questions—or simply her steady, nonthreatening personality—might have freed Noura to speak more openly. A person so comfortable Noura fell asleep in her car. Pairing Noura with Connie Justice, a seemingly sympathetic female, in those crucial hours after her mother's discovery was in hindsight pitch perfect:

Witness Statement

Incident #0506002215Me
Type of Report: Homicide
Location: 5001 NewHaven
Date: 06-05-2005

This is the statement of: Noura Grace Jackson

Age: 18
D.O.B: 03-17-1987
Sex: Female
Race: White
SSN: unknown
Home Address: 5001 Newhaven
Education: 11th Grade @ Ridgeway
Occupation: student
Employer: Ridgeway High

Next of Kin/Emergency Contact: Randolph Reeves (uncle)

This statement is being taken at the Homicide Office, 201 Poplar, Room 11-21 on Sunday, June 05, 2005 at 0835 hours.

This statement is relative to the Homicide complaint of Jennifer Jackson which occurred at 5001 Newhaven on Sunday, June 05, 2005.

Q: What is your relationship to Jennifer Jackson?
A: She's my mother.

Q: Do you live at 5001 Newhaven?
A: Yes.

Q: How long have you lived at 5001 Newhaven?
A: Five years.

Q: When is the last time you spoke with your mom?
A: At 12:10 this morning.

Q: Where were you when you last spoke with your mom?
A: At Perry's house.

Q: Did you go to the Italian Fest last evening on Saturday night?
A: Yes.

Q: Is that in Marquette Park?
A: Yes.

Q: Who is Perry?
A: He's like my boyfriend, but we've been on and off lately, but we've been on and off for about a year.

Q: Where does Perry live?
A: In Germantown.

Q: How did you get to Perry's?
A: We were at Carter's house after the Italian Fest, then we drove to another party in Germantown, then we went to Perry's house.

Q: Does Perry live with his parents or alone?
A: His parents.

Q: When you spoke with your mom, did you use Perry's phone or your cell?
A: My cell phone.

Q: What conversation did you have with your mom?
A: She told me that she was going to bed and I needed to go to church in the morning and that it started at 10:00 instead of 9:00.

Q: How long did you talk to her?
A: I don't know, like 5 minutes if that.

Q: What did you do after you spoke with your mom?
A: Hung out at Perry's a little longer . . . maybe 30 minutes, then they took me back to my car and I went out and got cigarettes, then I went to Taco Bell, then I realized that I didn't have my wallet, I called Perry to ask him to look around his house for it, so I went back to Carter's and found my wallet, then I bought gas, I have a receipt for that. Then I drove to Cordova to Eric Whittakers [Whitaker's], but decided to head on home, we talked for a minute though. I was talking to Andrew Hammack on the phone. He was going to stop by my house and see my kitten and we were supposed to talk. I was supposed to call him when I got home, but I found what I found and I didn't get to call him.

Q: What time did you arrive home?
A: I have no idea. I was on my way back from Eric's house and it was between 4 and 5.

Q: When you got home, did you go immediately inside?

A: When I was driving, I had been smoking a cigarette and when I got there I was walking to the front door and I stood there for a minute and took the last few drags and then I threw my butt in the side of the flower bed.

Q: When you got home, which door did you use to enter the house?
A: The front door . . . the door I have the key to . . . there's no keys to any of the metal doors.

Q: Was the door locked?
A: Yes.

Q: From the front door, where did you go?
A: In the kitchen to get my cat, she was in the corner and crying. I stepped on something that cracked and I realized there was glass all over the floor.

Q: Where did you go next?
A: So then I walked into my mom's room and I took the basket off of her head . . . I tried to talk to her, but she wouldn't talk, then I tried to feel a pulse, I kept shaking her, then I ran out of the front door to the neighbor's house and got them and I was screaming and they followed me back and then I ran into the sunroom to call the cops from the land phone and then I went in the kitchen and sat on the floor and I was holding my cat screaming just waiting for them to get there.

Q: What neighbor's house did you run to?
A: The Cox [Cocke's] across the street.

Q: Who came back with you?
A: Joe and his wife Rachael.

Q: Did you turn on any light switches?
A: Yes, the light in the hallway, the light in my mom's bathroom was on, which I thought was weird, I don't remember if I flipped on the light in my mom's room . . . I don't remember because it all happened so fast.

Q: Did you use the phone in the sunroom to call police?
A: Yes.

Q: What did you notice that was unusual when you went in the house?
A: There was cracked glass in the kitchen, my mom's lights from her bathroom was on and her bedroom door was open. She usually sleeps with her door closed.

Q: Could you tell where the glass came from that was on the kitchen floor?
A: The windows in the door.

Q: When your mom goes to bed, where does she keep her purse, cell phone or any other valuables?
A: All on the left side of her bed, there's a space between the desk and the bed and she keeps it in the space right beside her bed.

Q: When you arrived home, were you alone?
A: Yes.

Q: Did anyone come over to your house before you went in and found your mom?
A: No.

Q: Describe your car.
A: It's a Jeep Cherokee, silver.

Q: What valuables does your mom have?
A: She had a really nice cell phone and she usually had cash and stuff in her wallet.

Q: Describe the cell phone.
A: A high tech cell phone . . . Burberry or something. She can use it at work, she's in the bond business.

Q: Have you had any arguments or disagreements with your mom recently?
A: Only the same kind that teenagers and mothers do. We were out of town a week or two ago and Perry, my ex-boyfriend threw a party at my house.

Q: Were you out of town with your mom?
A: Yes.

Q: Why was Perry allowed at the house?
A: Because he was feeding the dog.

Q: How did your mom find out?
A: The neighbors . . . they called the cops because there were so many kids there.

Q: Who did your mom get mad at?

A: She was disappointed with Perry cause she trusted him.

Q: Does your mom have a boyfriend?
A: Not anymore, she had an off and on again boyfriend, this week they're broken up.

Q: What's his name?
A: Mark Irving [Irvin].

Q: Would you recognize Mark's picture?
A: Yes, they dated three years.

Q: While you went to the Italian fest, what was your mom doing last night?
A: She was at a wedding.

Q: Who did she go with?
A: Jimmy Tool [Tual].

Q: Do you know Jimmy?
A: Yes.

Q: Would you recognize Jimmy's picture?
A: Yes.

Q: Do you have any blood on your clothes?
A: Yes, on my shoes.

Q: Where did you touch your mom?
A: On her arms and face.

Q: You've got a cut on your left hand near the thumb, how did that happen?
A: While we were at Italian Fest, I went both nights at the pavilion . . . this happened Friday night. People were breaking beer bottles, I tripped and fell over it. My mom got this stuff for me which is like adhesive stuff and you put it on and when you take it off there's no scar . . . it's New Skin. People were busting beer bottles, there was people drunk everywhere. I also bruised my right hand.

Q: When was the last time you spoke with Perry last night?
A: When I called him about my wallet.

Q: Do you know what time that was?
A: No.

Q: Who took you back to your car from Perry's house?
A: Richard Raines, Sophie Coolie [Cooley] and Brook[e] Thompson were in the car too.

Q: What kind of car does Richard have?
A: A 2005 Z71 black Tahoe.

Q: Do you know Richard's number?
A: It's in my cell phone.

Q: Do you know were Richard lives?
A: In East Memphis with his mother, I haven't been to his new house.

Q: What were the seating arrangements in Richard's vehicle.

A: Sophie was in the front seat and me and Brook[e] were in the back.

Q: Does your mom keep any weapons in the house?
A: No.

Q: When your mom sleeps at night, what does she usually wear?
A: A big T-shirt, sometimes she wears underwear.

Q: Would your mom's boyfriend, Mark Irving [Irvin] spend the night with her?
A: Yes, lots of times.

Q: Has Mark and your mom been involved in an argument lately?
A: They fight all the time.

Q: What is Mark like?
A: I hate him, I think he's a really big selfish asshole, he uses his front as a preacher to make people think he's nice.

Q: Are their arguments physical?
A: No, heated words.

Q: Has Mark ever hit your mom before?
A: Not to my knowledge.

Q: Do you know who's wedding your mom went to or where it was?
A: I don't know whose, but it was at Calvary.

Q: How long has your mom known James Tool [Tual]?
A: He's just a socialite that would take my mom out when she and Mark broke up . . . she's known him a long time . . . she's known him longer than she's known Mark . . . her old roommate used to date him.

Q: What kind of car does Mark have?
A: A green Toyota maybe . . .

Q: What kind of car does James have?
A: I don't know.

Q: Did you use any other doors this morning other than the front door?
A: I opened up the door going into the sunroom, I think I made sure it was latched, I don't know if I touched it or not.

Q: Do you remember anywhere else in the house that you touched while you were inside?
A: I remember that while I was using the land line to call the police, there were some beach towels near the phone that I used to wipe my hands off . . . there sitting on top of the chair near the phone. I looked for the cordless phone first, I think I opened up the door to my room, but I couldn't find it, so I ran to the sunroom.

Q: Sgt. Justice showed you a picture of Mark Irvin, is this the Mark that you know?
A: Yes.

Q: Sgt. Justice showed you a picture of James Tual, is this the James that you know?

A: Yes.

Q: Do you know of anyone else that may want to harm your mom?
A: Warner Kotchman works at NBC Capital's Interest Group with my mom. He and my mom got into it over an account that was on his list that she called on. Management awarded it to her because they wanted to do business with her. This was maybe a month ago. They're not friends anymore.

Q: Is there anything else you would like to add to this statement that would aid us with this investigation?
A: No.

Q: Was this statement given freely and voluntarily, without any threats or promises?
A: Yes.

Q: Can you read and write without aid of eyeglasses?
A: Yes.

Q: I will now ask you to read this statement and if you find it to be true and correct, initial the bottom of each page except the last, sign the last page. Do you understand?
A: Yes.

After the statement, Justice took a full set of Noura's fingerprints and a saliva sample. (She also requested saliva swabs from Andrew Hammack and Mark Irvin.) Then, in a small, private interview room, she took photos of Noura:

what she was wearing, her nails, hands, the bandage. Justice asked her how bad the cut was and if she needed stitches. She felt Noura did not want her to lift the bandage—more a piece of tape with no absorption pad—but she never directly asked to see the injury. Noura declined stitches and, in Justice's opinion, "seemed uncomfortable talking about the cut on her hand."

When they returned to New Haven a little after noon, Justice helped Noura find the kitty in the garage that had seemingly dominated her thoughts all morning. She gave Noura her purse, keys, cell phone, and told her she could take her Jeep, but Justice kept the New Balance tennis shoes with blood on them that Noura was wearing. Noura's aunt Grace felt Noura showed a strange affinity for the tennis shoes. Grace could not imagine why Noura wanted shoes with blood on them that were part of the crime scene.

Justice stayed at the home another three hours and during that time talked with Helldorfer. "Well," he said, "I know I told Connie when she brought [Noura] back to the scene, 'Connie, she did it.' Connie said, 'No, I got a statement from her.' But she didn't know what I did." Helldorfer felt that he'd absorbed enough at New Haven that morning—Noura's reluctance to sign the consent to search and the "staged" break-in—to look carefully at Noura as a suspect. He had yet to share all this information with Connie Justice.

Justice spoke with Noura two additional times. She called her the next morning for phone numbers of people Noura was with the night before. She also tried to clarify Noura's time line, especially regarding the trip to Taco Bell she mentioned in her statement. The morning of June 6 Noura wouldn't confirm the location of the Taco Bell. This went on until Noura broke down and told her she hadn't been there at all but was "driving around smoking a bowl of weed."

Some time later in the investigation Justice received a phone call from Noura. She wanted to know if there were any breaks in the case.

Justice's testimony helped persuade one of the jurors of Noura's guilt. She believed Noura felt her mother's murder "was just something that had to be done." For her, the message of Noura's nap in the detective's car was "I'm done. I'm in a safe place. It's a done deal now."

Dr. Karen Chancellor

In each of Jennifer's hands the medical examiner found a loose strand of hair. Those strands of hair she noted to be long and blonde.

Valerie Corder: And did you analyze the loose hair from the right hand?
DNA Expert Qadiayyah Debman: No I did not.
Corder: Did you analyze the hair from the left hand?
Debman: No I did not.—Trial Testimony Day Seven

A wisp of a woman with close-cropped, dark hair and glasses, Dr. Karen Elizabeth Chancellor, the chief medical examiner for Shelby County, began her testimony as most expert witnesses did by reciting degrees and credentials. It seemed an unnecessary ritual in her case as both the prosecution and defense were noticeably deferential toward her. It was fascinating to imagine what might have drawn her to such a profession, her days spent determining what tragedy or malicious intent ended a life. Chancellor, a veteran at courtroom testimony, related in an understated delivery what Jennifer Jackson's autopsy revealed about the nature of her death.

Chancellor's office received Jennifer's body late Sunday afternoon wrapped in a sealed white bag covered with a white sheet. Partially dried blood covered most of her body. Because autopsies generally are performed during the day, the procedure was delayed until Monday, June 6. The initial step in her process was to examine the exterior body. First, Chancellor cleaned the blood and noted the multiple sharp-force injuries. She listed fifty to fifty-one stab wounds—which are longer in depth than can be seen on the outside—and a number of cuts. Cuts are longer on the surface of body than a stab wound, which is deeper.

Jennifer's body was measured and weighed: seventy inches or five-foot-ten-inches tall and 166 pounds. A known blood sample was taken from the victim and placed on a card. This would be used to compare blood samples found at the crime scene. Chancellor completed a sexual assault kit (negative) and collected hair samples and nail clippings. The underside of the nails were scraped for evidence. The loose hairs Chancellor recovered from Jennifer's hands were turned over to investigators. When a juror asked if the strands were sent to the Tennessee Bureau of Investigation (TBI), Chancellor answered that she didn't know. She had given them to the police department. Astonishingly, those hairs that could very well have been from the assailant were never tested.

On day seven of the trial, prior to Chancellor taking the stand, the defense and prosecution reviewed autopsy pictures. Judge Craft ruled on what photographs would be permitted. He warned family members of the images to come and said he would not allow excessively gruesome photographs to be viewed for fear of influencing the jury. From the outset of Chancellor's testimony, the change in

Noura was notable in her emotions. She cried and looked away from the displayed visuals. Chancellor worked from her own diagrams of the front and back of a female body and the actual autopsy photographs using an overhead projector. She stressed that she could not determine the exact order of the stab wounds, nor could she determine the position or size of the person wielding the knife.

The deep wounds were to the front torso. The chest wounds were made from a ninety-degree angle—or from straight above the body—and went through the sternum and struck the heart. "It doesn't take a lot of force [to penetrate the breastbone] if you have a sharp instrument with a fine point on it. It didn't take a lot of force, though it would take more than if it was soft tissue," Chancellor said. The maximum depth was six inches, so the knife, or one of the knives if there were two, was at least that long. The knife or knives' width, she estimated, was one-half to three-fourths of an inch. The orientation of the sharp edge of the knife was up toward the head for wounds to the chest and abdomen.

The right and left ventricles of Jennifer's heart were perforated. Her lungs were damaged as well as the liver and stomach. Chancellor determined the damaged lungs led to internal bleeding and approximately a liter of blood had drained into the chest cavity. That would be a fifth of the average amount in person's body. The abdominal wounds were made by downward thrusts toward Jennifer's feet, and Chancellor believed those were some of the last wounds inflicted because not as much internal blood had collected there. The amount of blood in the body cavity is the only way to estimate the order or timing of the stab wounds.

Both the abdominal and chest wounds were consistent with cuts made with a smooth knife blade or single-edge knife, the most common kind of knife. One such blow went completely through the abdominal aorta. The stab wounds on Jennifer's back pierced the skin and tissue but did not penetrate vital organs. "I can't tell you the position of the assailant, but I can tell you the position of the knife," Chancellor said. "It was held downwards."

The right and left sides of Jennifer's neck were covered with cut marks and stabs. Seven mostly superficial wounds on the right side of her neck and seven or eight on the left. Muscle tissue, the cricoid cartilage, and Adam's apple were damaged. Even Jennifer's face had not escaped the assailant. Injuries to her face included her right cheek, a deep vertical cut on her forehead that went through to the skull, and a patterned wound on the chin probably caused by a serrated edge. Chancellor testified that the cuts on the neck and chin were from a serrated edge; that she couldn't think of anything other than a serrated knife that would cause those types of wounds. She said the wounds could be from two different knives or an unusual knife that had a serrated edge on one side and a smooth blade on the other. "If I had a weapon," she added, "I could compare it."

Chancellor confirmed that the right side of Jennifer's body showed fewer wounds—Noura said in her witness statement that her mother kept her phone and valuables on the left side of her bed—and that the wounds on the right were generally downward and toward the left side of her body. Yet there was a through-and-through wound on the upper edge of her right arm and the wrist, palm, and fingers of her right hand revealed several defensive cuts that indicated Jennifer tried to grab the knife while she was being stabbed.

The toxicology report was consistent with Jimmy Tual's account of Jennifer's alcohol consumption that night. She would have tested .07 on a Breathalyzer. Chancellor noted that such a blood alcohol content might result in diminished coordination, a slower response time, and perhaps mild euphoria. Though Jennifer was tested for marijuana, cocaine, opiates, barbiturates, and others, the only drug found in her body was Benadryl. Chancellor told Corder she had not been told about the Trojan condom wrapper found on the bedroom floor near the headboard and bedside table. From a postmortem exam, however, she could not rule out the possibility that Jennifer may have had consensual sex that night.

Chancellor concluded Jennifer died from multiple stab wounds and officially ruled her death a homicide. She estimated the time of death to be twenty-four to forty-eight hours prior to her examination on June 6 at 9:30 a.m., and further stated there was no way to tell the exact time of death. Rigor mortis takes between two and eight hours to occur. In fact, Chancellor said, the estimated time presented by investigators—between 12:30 a.m. and 5:10 a.m.—was consistent with the science and actually narrower than her own time frame.

The medical examiner's testimony confirmed Helldorfer's insight that "You could tell there was a lot that happened in there." On this, the prosecution and defense agreed. In her closing argument, Valerie Corder said, "Jennifer fought for her life in a brutal, vicious knife fight," and that "The crime scene indicated a fight and a struggle." Besides the knife injuries there were bruises. The bruise on the left side of Jennifer's head was classified as a recent, blunt-force injury. A blunt object rather than sharp one also bruised her right arm and right leg.

If you stood in the doorway of Jennifer's bedroom, you would have seen that her bedside table was on the left side of the bed and beside the table a pair of corner windows. She kept her valuables tucked close by—between the bed and her nightstand—and, one would think, slept safely ensconced in that far corner from the door. How had she managed such mobility—from that edge of the room to near the middle—when probably the first wounds inflicted were fatal?

Jennifer's astounding struggle for her life, as she attempted to fight or flee her assailant, or both, ended at the foot of her bed. She somehow made it off the left side of the bed where she slept, to the floor, and on her final collapse, wound up parallel to the footboard. Her feet were touching the left bedpost, and her head was near the right bedpost, and closer to the bedroom door.

At the Madison

"We felt she had brutally and savagely murdered our sister, and for her to walk away with a pot of money would be the biggest travesty of all."—Grace France

Eric's eldest sister, Grace, called him about Jennifer's murder. Slightly later Noura called him as well. "She sounded like she was dead inside."—Eric Sherwood

Grace was home in Atlanta on June 5 when a phone call from her niece shattered her Sunday morning. "Something terrible has happened to Mom," Noura told her before handing the phone over to her neighbor. Then, a highly emotional Sheila Cocke blurted out "Jennifer has been stabbed to death! She's been murdered!"

With that ghastly news hurtled at her, Grace was burdened with the unhappy role of messenger. She called her brother Eric who lives in Memphis, and Cindy, who had arrived in Portugal on vacation with her family the night before. An hour flight separates Atlanta from Memphis, and Grace was in town Monday. Cindy arrived Tuesday, and the three siblings were confronted with the shock and pain of this sudden parting. Their sister was a murder victim; she was gone from them forever.

Grace arranged rooms for Cindy and her husband, Frank, herself, and, they assumed, Noura. The suite at the Madison, a fashionable boutique hotel in downtown Memphis, could accommodate them all. Grace's first reaction when she got the news was to situate Noura with family, get her to their cousin, Randolph Reeve's home, but Noura resisted over the phone on Sunday, saying "I don't feel comfortable going to Randolph's." Grace was surprised—the family often had gathered at Randolph's home—and said, "It was the first I'd heard of that." In her witness statement with Detective Justice, Noura listed Randolph Reeves as her uncle and "next of kin/emergency contact." Noura also declined to stay at the hotel Monday night with Grace telling her she preferred to be with her friends even though her aunt admonished that she needed to be with family.

Dana Fredrick quickly came to Noura's aid as she so often had in the past. She was at early church June 5 when her daughter Lindsey called to tell her about Jennifer. Dana immediately drove to New Haven to comfort Noura. Later she tried in vain to speak with Grace at the Madison. She left at least three messages in which she explained her relationship with Noura and offered to have Noura stay at her house, but her calls were never returned.

While Grace knew from conversations with Jennifer that there were problems with Noura, Cindy's observations were firsthand and fresh. Noura and Jennifer's Memorial Day weekend visit had occurred only a week prior to the murder. Cindy's head must have spun as she recalled the drama: the fight over the party at New Haven; the mother and daughter's harsh exchange of words; and Noura's sullen and unresponsive mood. Those incidences would now be magnified and loom large. With Jennifer gone, Cindy no doubt realized the difficulty of dealing with her rebellious niece fell to Grace, Eric, and herself.

When Cindy reached Memphis her first questions were for Noura. "What happened that night?" she asked. "I heard you were at the house because [Perry] said you were outside the house smoking." Noura insisted she wasn't home but was with another boy—the mysterious Chris whom Noura said Perry disliked. Cindy continued to probe for answers and more details as she tried to come to terms with her sister's death. Did Noura know who could have done this? Noura finally said she couldn't talk about it. "It's too painful," she told her aunt.

On Tuesday, Grace and Cindy took Noura shopping for clothes and essentials. Grace remembered Noura wearing a heavy, gray polar fleece that was "very oversized for her" and flip-flops. They took her shopping at Marshall's department store for nightgowns and clothing. The sisters were puzzled by Noura's selections for the hot June weather. Every item she purchased was long sleeved.

That night Noura stayed with them, and they were as alarmed by her despondent and erratic behavior as Regina Hunt had been earlier in the day. While Cindy and Grace went to dinner, Noura took the $800.00 they had given her to arrange her mother's cremation. "Noura was insistent that she do it because [Perry Brasfield's father] owned the crematorium," Grace said. She and Cindy were prepared to go; "We wanted to go," Grace said, but Noura remained adamant. However, family members wound up making the trip anyway because Noura couldn't answer questions like her mother's place of birth and her birth date. Jennifer's funeral was three days later.

Cindy described those days at the Madison as "very blurry. My sister had just died." Making matters more difficult were the unavoidable demands foisted upon them: a funeral to plan, a murder investigation to assist, and a niece having suicidal outbursts. All of which created a whirlpool of grief and suspicion.

Teenage antics were one thing but when Noura kept saying she wanted to kill herself, the family realized she needed professional help. Three days after Jennifer's death, on the recommendation of a therapist, Noura was admitted to Charter Lakeside Behavioral Health System, a name synonymous in the Memphis area with drug problems and mental health issues. (With the exception of one slip by Eric on the witness stand, Charter Lakeside was referred to in the presence of the jury as the "hospital.")

Wednesday at Lakeside, Grace recalled Noura wearing a long-sleeved white shirt. "She was very down," Grace said, "and she didn't want to be with us." Both Grace and Cindy sensed her distance. Some friends, including Andrew Hammack, sat with Noura as she prepared to voluntarily admit herself. Noura told Andrew the hospital stay would be good for her; it would be good "to get [her] mind right."

If Noura had ideas Lakeside would be a sanctuary from the reality of a murder investigation, they were soon extinguished. Two days after her admittance, Noura's aunts picked her up for her mother's funeral. Jennifer's memorial service was held Friday, June 10, at 11:00 a.m. following a one-hour visitation at the Episcopal church she and Noura attended. A grieving crowd filled the reception area of the Church of the Holy Communion where Jennifer had attended Reverend Jerry Harber's Sunday school class every week. He told *Commercial Appeal* reporter Aimee Edmondson, "[Jennifer] was a beautiful person, both inside and out. I seldom saw her without a smile."

Jimmy Tual recalled the service as "packed." Many of Noura's friends attended along with Jennifer's. For Tual the service was "surreal." Not even a full week earlier, he and Jennifer had gone to a wedding together.

Jennifer had told friends that after Noura was grown she wanted to go sailing. Her friend Amy Allen in Atlanta remembered those words, "She wanted to be on a yacht, by herself, traveling the world."

For Noura, a very bad day was about to become worse. Following the emotional upheaval of her mother's funeral, unexpected visitors at Lakeside reminded her that as far as police were concerned she was more than merely related to the victim, Noura was the object of their intense interest. After a brief shopping trip to Target with Cindy and Grace following Jennifer's service, Noura returned to Lakeside to find police officers waiting. Crime Scene Officer Kay Turnmire and Detective Connie Justice, with whom Noura already was familiar from her witness statement, were there to photograph and document the condition of Noura's overall body. To do so, Noura was asked to undress. The seventeen photos included several close ups of the cut—now healing—on her left hand, her stomach, back, side of buttocks, inside and outside of thighs, a small bruise on her left thigh, and the top and bottom—different angles—of her feet.

Judging by the photographs taken that day, Noura's emotional health had a long and rocky road ahead. Wearing a black, sleeveless shirt—not quite waist length—a short, pleated black-and-white-striped skirt with large white buttons above the side slit, and thin-strapped, black sandals with a moderate heel, the full-body photograph showed Noura's unkempt hair swirling across her face. She had a dark summer tan, and her stomach hung over a bit where the shirt didn't meet the waistband of her skirt. Noura's disheveled image and her sad, downcast eyes reflected the earth-shattering recent events. All the attention she paid to her hair, makeup, and clothes—the hours spent with friends dressing and getting ready—belonged to another lifetime.

Noura stayed about a month at Lakeside, and with her aunts back home, her uncle Eric would visit her twice a week. He also wanted answers from Noura and confronted her about Jennifer. He asked if she knew anything about her mother's death, "She just put her head down on the table and didn't want to talk about it," he said. Eventually she volunteered that she cut her hand when she jumped a barbed wire fence at Italian Fest. Roughly a week after the funeral he started probing again. This time Noura told him that "she burned it."

Despite his suspicions about Noura's evasiveness, Eric was there for her upon her release, and she spent the first night after Lakeside with him. Cindy said she made many trips to Memphis but none that she recalled during the month Noura was at Lakeside or the month she lived alone in her apartment. Her trips to Memphis became frequent after Noura'a arrest.

The realities of Noura's financial dependency dictated that she and Grace talk much more than they had in years, often once or twice a week. At this time Jennifer's sisters were supporting Noura, having finally found her an apartment they could agree upon. Still money continued to be a source of friction. Cindy and Grace felt Noura didn't appreciate the situation, and they tried to explain that money was tight with Jennifer's estate inaccessible. They figured what they considered a fair sum for groceries and gas, but the money was going faster than they felt it should. Grace said they attempted to reign in Noura's spending but she persisted, buying a dog and exceeding the budget they provided for living expenses. "A friend of mine has been working out with a personal trainer and I'd really like to do that," Noura told Grace. Her aunt seemed to consider that an exorbitant and strange request. Grace reiterated to Noura that funds were limited.

Grace and Cindy's involvement in Noura's day-to-day devolved after she was evicted from the apartment they found for her. About a month passed between her losing the apartment and her arrest in September when both aunts received calls from her.

When she called Cindy from the police station, Noura might have hoped for comfort or support, but instead she faced familiar questions.

"Noura," Cindy queried, "tell me where you were and who you were with when your mother was killed."

"I don't know."

Cindy repeated the question.

"I don't know."

"And I never heard from her again," Cindy said.

Cindy maintained she "would have gotten [Noura] lawyers or anything she needed if she had an alibi and could prove to me where she was and who she was with when Jennifer was murdered."

When Noura called Grace she asked for her help. She had been babysitting, and the parents owed her some money, she explained. Would Grace contact the parents and get the money for her? Grace was having none of it. "Before I'll help you, we—the family—have a lot of questions. What about that cut on your hand?"

"Any doctor would tell you, Aunt Grace, that it's a burn. I burned it cooking macaroni and cheese," Noura explained. "She said it very convincingly," Grace added.

In the days following Jennifer's death there were many obligations to be met, though nothing more onerous than cleaning out the New Haven home. Besides an above-average house full of stuff—walls filled top to bottom with storage bins—the garage was overflowing, and there were additional off-site storage units. Most of this extensive clearing out occurred after Noura's arrest. Cindy and Grace eventually moved the four or five off-site units into the house and sorted through them as well. Those contents included items from the convenience store belonging to Noura's father, Nazmi, including an ATM machine. The sisters organized an estate sale, and the proceeds went into a fund for Noura if she was acquitted.

Even before she was incarcerated, Noura steadfastly refused to return to the New Haven home. That left Cindy and Grace wondering what personal items Noura would want to keep. They turned to Bill Shelton, and he agreed to care for Noura's possessions. One day when he was at the house collecting Noura's things he found a discarded shopping list on the street, presumably for the trash pickup. The list included Band-Aids, Durex condoms, and "Boo," a reference to the family dog.

During Grace's cross-examination she was asked to identify her sister's writing, so the list could be admitted as evidence. Then Art Quinn read aloud two tender notes Jennifer had composed for Noura in the spring of 2005, a Valentine's Day card that said "You have so much love to give," and a card commemorating her eighteenth birthday. Tears sprang to Noura's eyes when the cards were read.

Jennifer's handwriting was quite distinct. "She wrote beautiful calligraphy," Grace said, "a beautiful form of penmanship." In the end, the undated shopping list did little for the defense, even though it referenced Durex, a different brand of condom than the Trojan found near Jennifer's body in her bedroom. And it added confusion to Noura's cut. It had happened earlier, the defense implied, and her mother had purchased Band-Aids for her. The evidentiary value of Jennifer's list was low, but the cards introduced a softer aspect of her personality: the intricate, perfected penmanship she used to craft endearing sentiments to the daughter she loved.

If Grace thought Noura's requests for a decent apartment and a personal trainer were excessive, defense attorney Quinn seemed to feel the same way about Grace and Cindy's stays at the Madison. Quinn's testy cross-examination of Grace hit on many family stress lines. He pressed her on her closeness to Jennifer. Grace admitted she had seen Jennifer only twice in the past two years: in 2003 at their mother's funeral, and in 2004 they took a trip to New York together. Jennifer had never met Grace's one-year-old child.

Quinn kept the pressure on. Why wasn't Grace in Jennifer's wedding or Jennifer in either of Grace's two weddings? Grace explained that her first wedding was a small chapel ceremony with only one bridesmaid. And her second wedding created tension between Cindy, who didn't support what she considered to be a "too hasty" marriage, and herself. Rather than have one sister without the other, Grace elected to ask neither.

Quinn's quizzical expression and acerbic tone when he asked about the sisters' fondness for staying at the Madison—a hotel he described as "expensive"—let the courtroom and especially the jury know he found the hotel an extravagance. Three and a half years of pretrial motions, appeals, and delays meant many trips to Memphis for Cindy and Grace. The Madison was another opportunity for the defense to tweak their position of financial motivation on the part of Jennifer's siblings.

Yet the sisters' situation, with an intense need for privacy, made the Madison an ideal if pricey choice. Jennifer's murder and Noura's arrest had excited intense curiosity in Memphis. The discretion of the Madison staff which is used to high-profile patrons ensured a buffer against possibly unwelcome intrusiveness. The hotel opened in 2002 after extensive renovation of the 1906 Tennessee Trust Building. The once deteriorating fourteen-story building was converted into 110 luxury rooms (costing the owners $170,000 per room). Preservation of the exterior's original ornate styling included the architects' signature scroll pattern.

Mohamad Hakimian, managing partner of the Madison said in an August 20, 2006, interview with Michael Sheffield *(Memphis Business Journal)* that the Madison's clientele isn't the traveler who is looking for frequent flyer miles. "A lot of business travelers take advantage of those benefits so when they go on vacation, they can travel or stay for free," he says. "We're not going to get those people and we don't go after them."

The Madison caters to business travelers who prefer personalized service and first-class attention. "We wanted to create an intimate environment where we could recognize guests by name and they could recognize staff by name," Hakimian said. According to Sheffield, the private nature of the hotel has attracted celebrities who are looking for a nice, quiet stay in Memphis. Visiting NBA teams stay there. Celebrities Lisa Marie and Priscilla Presley, Bono, Cher, Steven Tyler, Boz Scaggs, and Joe Montana have also been guests.

A recent notable stay at the Madison during August of 2011 involved two of the West Memphis Three. The rooftop venue provided the backdrop for Damien Echols and Jason Baldwin's release party. The two men, along with Jessie Misskelley, had spent the previous eighteen years in prison for the murder conviction of three young boys in West Memphis, Arkansas, located just across the Mississippi River from Memphis. The case attracted national and international attention.

The Friday afternoon of their liberation, August 19, Baldwin and Echols were whisked away in a Mercedes flanked by the bodyguards of one of their celebrity supporters, Eddie Vedder, of the rock band Pearl Jam. More than fifty people, including Dixie Chicks' singer Natalie Maines, joined the celebration. Vedder and Maines sang together in honor of the hard-fought victory, closing out the evening with Neil Young's "Rockin' in the Free World."

Spottswood

"Are they here for me?"—Noura to Rebecca Robertson

In the days and weeks following her mother's murder in June until the September day when she was arrested, Noura led a vagabond existence. She was a patient at Charter Lakeside Hospital; she lived briefly in her own apartment; and she spent nights on friends' couches or in their guest rooms, essentially living out of her vehicle for clothing—"a wardrobe on wheels" as one blogger aptly described it.

Dana Fredrick opened her home to Noura where she spent several days after her release from Lakeside. To Dana, Noura was still "very sweet," though unusually quiet and depressed. Dana came home one day to find Noura asleep on her couch still wearing her cowboy boots. Dana saw her as merely going through the motions of living. "Noura," she said, "was far from her usual happy self and not very talkative."

But of the various places Noura stayed, Rebecca Robertson's home is the most puzzling. Robertson worked as an assistant property manager at the Quail Ridge Apartment Complex in Bartlett, a suburb of Memphis, where Noura's uncle Eric handled apartment maintenance. Robertson first met Noura at Jennifer's funeral which Robertson attended because of her friendship with Eric. She eventually allowed Noura to stay with her and her six-year-old daughter for over a month until Noura moved into her own place.

The subtext of her generosity might have been an interest in Eric Sherwood. Otherwise, it is a little hard to understand such hospitality for a near stranger. Robertson's kind gesture soon confirmed the oft-quoted adage, "no good deed goes unpunished." If Noura wasn't the houseguest from hell, Roberson's depiction put her very close.

Robertson said her prescription medication was disappearing. On one occasion Noura offered to pick up her Lortab prescription from the pharmacy after Robertson's dental work, but Noura said she left the pills in someone else's car, and they were never recovered. Then, Robertson's Xanax went missing.

Noura's random comings and goings were also a problem for the single mother. Robertson didn't actually see much of Noura, and when she was there, she was sleeping late. Most of the time Noura was out with friends, dropping in to sleep and shower. But then she started bringing friends to Robertson's apartment and coming in late. Robertson said she was trying to comfort Noura, though she eventually asked her to stop the disruptive behavior. Besides losing her own privacy, it was difficult for her daughter's schedule.

Robertson noticed the hand injury almost immediately—Noura told her it happened at Italian Fest—and offered to apply some ointment to avoid scarring. Noura responded to her offer of assistance as she had to others. "She didn't want my help, and she didn't want to talk about it," Robertson asserted.

It must have been a relief when Noura moved into her own two-bedroom apartment at Quail Ridge. An apartment she was able to secure with the help of her family even though Noura had no income, and hers was the only name on the lease. The signed lease agreement stipulated no late night, loud parties or pets, both of which Noura promptly disregarded, leaving Robertson with a new set of problems. The parties in Noura's apartment started about a week after she moved in, and soon there were noise complaints from neighbors. She told Robertson she couldn't control her friends' behavior, but naturally that didn't solve the problem. And Noura had acquired a dog, a Rottweiler, despite the no pet policy.

Noura most likely knew she had some leeway with her uncle working there. Eric had helped Noura get settled. She had not wanted to return to New Haven even to pick out furniture or clothes, so Eric did both for her, bringing them to the apartment. He was concerned about how Noura was spending her time, and he suggested she get a job to "keep herself occupied." She told him she would go into the business of selling pills. And since he noticed various pills and drug paraphernalia around the apartment, he probably didn't dismiss the notion.

One day Noura was visiting with Robertson in her apartment office. There had been a disturbance with a tenant, and Robertson had called the police. She and Noura peered out the window together and Noura asked her, "Are they here for me?" A startled Robertson responded, "No, why would they be here for you?" It unsettled Robertson who said it was "kind of unnerving a little bit the *way* she spoke it. And she seemed really nervous. Very uncomfortable." She began to distance herself from Noura. After Noura received two or three warnings about the parties and her dog, they evicted her due to lease agreement violations. Robertson didn't allow her to sleep on her couch anymore and dropped all communication with Noura "for her and her daughter's well being."

Noura understood the police were investigating her; talking with her friends and people she knew. Yet that did not stop her from entertaining. She was the first of her group to have her own place and they took full advantage of the space. Almost everyone said they drank and smoked marijuana while they were there.

Andrew said after Jennifer's death Noura was "relieved. A different person. She was free and didn't have a curfew. She seemed concerned about her mother's death but glad not to have anyone to answer to."

Perry and Noura reconnected. They had sex, watched TV, hung out, used cocaine (which Noura supplied) and Lortab. Not one time during those days in her apartment, according to Perry, did they ever talk about Jennifer's murder. Only after Noura's arrest did Perry break his silence on the matter. He asked her what she was doing the night her mother died. She didn't say anything. "No words," Perry said.

It's hard to say if the group's partying intensified during the month Noura had the apartment. But if it wasn't more frequent, it certainly was no less. Besides Perry's visits, six additional friends who testified for the prosecution partied and even stayed overnight at Noura's apartment. Sophie described the apartment as a place to "Hang out with your friends unsupervised." On her two visits, there were about ten other people partying as well.

Kaole was concerned about Noura when he saw her eating Xanax bars and asked her about it. She told him that "it was to help ease [her] emotions and help [her] relax and calm down." He noted her bag of Lortabs, but he had one as well. Carter and Kirby both recalled smoking weed and drinking. Brooke only remembered one visit during the day with Sophie, though she was not sure why they went. Joey was one of the more frequent guests, citing about ten visits. "We drank a lot," he said, "beer, whiskey, and vodka." He saw Noura taking Lortab but said he tried to stay away from Lortab as well as cocaine. Christian Brothers High School performed drug tests and he didn't want to fail.

Evicted from her apartment and banished even from Robertson's couch, Noura spent the next few weeks of late summer and early fall staying with friends or at a couple's home for whom she was babysitting. For two days Noura went about her business unaware she had been charged with murder. On Tuesday, September 27, the Shelby County Grand Jury indicted her for first-degree murder, but she was not arrested until Thursday, September 29. Whether or not Noura sensed the impending doom as she drove up to a friend's house on Spottswood is unknown. There Memphis police swooped in and made the arrest, taking Noura first to 201 Poplar and later to Jail East.

Upon learning of Noura's arrest, Jennifer's friend in Atlanta, Amy Allen, said, "It brings an unbelievable sense of pain to learn that Jennifer's wonderful spirit and life were taken away by an unhappy daughter that (sic) she loved as much as she could."

Strange Beast

"Nice story. They showed you three receipts and a bunch of potheads and said it means Noura Jackson killed her mother."—Valerie Corder's closing argument

"Wait until the top of my head flies off, Judge."—Valerie Corder's reply when, as day two of the trial wound down, Judge Craft commented that she had been uncharacteristically quiet.

Faced with a prosecution able to assemble a fetching cast of characters exhibiting lots of misbehavior—partying, sex, drugs—it was no wonder there was a hint of frustration in Valerie Corder's voice during her closing argument. Hands down the prosecution had storytelling on their side. With visuals of key witnesses and participants on display in a PowerPoint presentation: the three beautiful sisters, the dramatic neighbor, his wife and mother, the teenage friends, and victim's friends, prosecutor Steve Jones moved through his case as methodically as a novelist outlines her or his plot. Whether fictional or factual, all the elements of a first class story were there.

Corder countered with her initial stance. The state had a good tale but no physical evidence. "Circumstantial evidence," she told the jury, "is a strange beast." She demonstrated just how strange by reassembling all the items of physical evidence introduced at trial and emphatically discarding each piece in one giant pile. And when an item landed, she reminded the jury it was free of Noura Jackson's blood or DNA.

"Let's put everything on this side of the courtroom that does not indicate Noura Jackson killed her mother," Corder said. "Basket, pillow, comforter: none of Noura Jackson's blood. Stepstool, bag, another pillow . . . bottom sheet, hoodie: none of Noura Jackson's blood."

The pile grew and grew until it was as high as the witness stand: dust ruffles, mattress pad, bed linens, a wallet, little blue bag, drinking glass from kitchen, white skirt, Walgreens bag, cigarette and lighter, business card, broken glass from the kitchen, doors, purse, various evidence envelopes, shoebox, shoes, bed finials, floor mats from the Jeep. A giant pile of evidence Corder argued that failed to connect Noura to her mother's murder.

The state, according to Corder, depicted Noura as a smart, remorseless, calculating murderer who brutally killed her mom without leaving a trace, "A diabolical, premeditated killer who is brilliant. Who leaves no blood or gets none of her mother's blood on her." But they also asked the jury to see her as a drugged out teenager. "You can't," she cautioned the jury, "have it both ways."

She referenced a photograph of Noura's hands on the overhead screen and asked if the hands looked like someone who had been in a violent knife fight, hand-to-hand combat? She flashed more photographs of Noura's hands. The pristine French manicure. "These aren't the hands of a child who killed her mother. The reason we know that is the scientific evidence tells us that."

The "nefarious plot" against Noura included significant character assassination, she insisted. Noura stayed out late, had sex, missed her curfews, took drugs, quarreled with her mom, and was an underage drinker. "Noura may be a bad girl," she said, "but she is not a murderer." Corder stressed that Noura's behavior was not atypical of many teenagers. She noted that Noura's crowd of friends—"pothead witnesses" as she termed them—did not have clear memories of events. "They were either mistaken, confused, or lying. They continued to associate with Noura, spend the night with her. Would they have done that if they thought she was a killer?"

Corder was drawn to Noura's case in part because she is a strong women's advocate. Tenacious, combative, some might say formidable, she was in command of the case's details down to the most obscure. Muddying the waters was part of her defense strategy, and she had plenty to work with. From the friends' memories colored by admitted drugs and alcohol use—"these children are not credible"—to a bungled handling of the crime scene—"a brutal, ugly, poor, incompetent investigation."

Tall, thin with sharp features, Corder wore rose-colored reading glasses and assumed a sometimes professorial tone in her closing. Surely everyone could see, as she did, how ludicrous this case was? "They do not have enough evidence to convict Noura of littering let alone murder," she boldly declared.

Reminding jurors again that not all evidence is equal, she repeated that "forensic evidence doesn't lie." She pointed to the pile of evidence she had assembled throughout her closing: "The scientific evidence is screaming at you from this pile over here. I know who did it. Find out."

For over an hour Corder methodically built the staggering pile of "unincriminating" evidence and ridiculed the CSI team, the investigation, and the prosecution's case against her client. "Before you take one more day of Noura Jackson's liberty," she stressed, the state must prove that Jennifer died when her daughter was in the house. If DNA doesn't matter, then why keep testing it? That's the most disingenuous argument of all—'it doesn't matter.'"

She reminded jurors of what was still missing—Jennifer's cell phone and house and car keys. Noura's Jeep, which had been towed by police and processed, had not a trace of blood on the floor mats or anywhere. It was a dirty, messy teenager's vehicle but yielded no evidence against her.

Police theorized that Noura dumped her bloody clothes and the murder weapon or weapons somewhere away from the house. Drops of Jennifer's blood were found outside on the front step.

"Well, if that were true," Corder said later on *48 Hours*, "then one would expect to find some of Noura's blood or some of Jennifer's blood in [Noura's Jeep] also. There was no blood in the vehicle."

When it was prosecuting attorney Amy Weirich's opportunity to respond to Corder, she zealously seized the moment. She leapt to her feet, looked directly at Noura and demanded loudly. 'Just tell *us* where you were! That's all *we're* asking Noura!" Then Corder and Quinn were on their feet, demanding a mistrial. Weirich said she merely was echoing the trial testimony from Noura's aunt Cindy. Cindy's actual testimony was "Noura, tell *me* where you were and who you were with when your mother was killed."

Before he allowed the prosecution to continue its closing rebuttal argument, Judge Craft addressed the jury and repeated the instructions he had given earlier in the day regarding the defendant's right not to testify: "I want to make a distinction here so you'll understand. . . . It's very important for all of you to understand that you cannot ever, ever hold anything against Noura for not testifying in this trial. . . . Also, at any time from the time of this alleged killing until today, Noura never has to talk to anyone about anything. She has an absolute right to remain silent, and it's up to the State to prove her guilt beyond a reasonable doubt. It's not up to anyone to prove they're innocent."

From there Weirich reiterated many of Jones' points while she moved theatrically about the room with her voice modulating from high tones to near whispers. "The last thing anyone wants to believe is that an eighteen-year-old girl could kill her mother." She asked the jury to clear their minds—impossible she knew—and imagine the picture of the perfect storm, "an enraged, out-of-control Noura Jackson snapping.

Do not be fooled, ladies and gentlemen. Do not be fooled into thinking that we have to tell you exactly when that premeditation was formed. We don't.

All you have to show is that it was there before the killing. How do we know that? Nobody walked in here and told you what was going in Noura's mind. Yeah, they did. Oh, yeah, they did. And it was ugly.

Give me my fucking money. Shhh, let's go inside. Can you believe my mom's going to get a restraining order on Perry? Can you believe my mom's drug testing me? Can you believe my mom won't let me continue to take drugs and whup it up and goof off in school? Can you believe it?

The nerve of a parent. A thirty-nine year old single (sic) mother, God love her, doing the best she can.

. . . .

The only thing that stood between the defendant and her freedom and her money and Perry Brasfield was her mother.

The prosecution chose to open its matricide case by concentrating on the argument Sheila Cocke had overheard between Noura and Jennifer. In an angry and forceful tone, Weirich loudly repeated Noura's alleged words. The defense believed Weirich so overreached in the volume and drama of her opening statement, that it, like her closing argument, amounted to prosecutorial misconduct.

"Alleged Prosecutorial Misconduct" accounted for fourteen pages of Justice Glenn's opinion on Noura's appeal of the guilty verdict. "The defendant asserts the prosecutorial misconduct began with the prosecution's opening statement and the phrase, 'Give me the f*cking money,' delivered 'to the jury in close proximity and at a deafening decibel level.' This statement came near the beginning of the State's opening statement, referring to the troubles brewing between the defendant and the victim. . . .

"As to this issue, we first must observe that, as to our reviewing the trial, we are limited to the transcript, which gives no hint as to the emotion or volume with which a statement is delivered. The State responds that the defendant has waived this issue by not objecting to the allegedly improper statement at the time it was made. We agree with the State that the defendant has waived this issue for appeal."

Regarding Weirich's paraphrase of Grace's quotation, "Just tell *us* where you were. That's all *we're* asking, Noura," Justice Glenn admonished that "there is risk to the State in rephrasing witness testimony, especially when it focuses on the fact that the defendant elected not to testify. The upshot of all this is that we cannot conclude that the prosecutor's argument, though certainly dramatic, was improper."

Justice Jeffrey S. Bivins and Justice Thomas T. Woodall disagreed. Justice Bivins composed the concurring opinion—joined by Justice Woodall—stating he could not agree with Justice Glenn. "I am compelled to conclude that the statement, indeed, did constitute an improper comment on the defendant's choice not to testify at trial. Although I do conclude that the remark was improper, to be entitled to a new trial, the improper remark must have affected the verdict of the jury," Bivins writes.

Bivins continues in his remarks to note that the trial was "long and complicated. . . . Despite a myriad of difficult evidentiary and other issues, the record before this court is of a relatively flawless trial. . . . The final factor for consideration is the relative strength or weakness of the case as a whole. This case clearly is primarily a circumstantial case. The overall proof, however, although not overwhelming, is relatively strong. Having considered all of the requisite factors, the final step is to review the totality of the findings and the weight to be given to each factor to determine whether the improper statement actually affected the verdict of the jury. Although this case presents a relatively close question, I conclude that the full analysis of these factors demonstrates that the improper statement did not affect the verdict of the jury. Accordingly, I, too, affirm the judgment of the trial court in this action."

Corder and Weirich both might have marveled that it was nothing they said or did in court that inspired the jury's "aha moment." Instead it was evidence the jury discovered during deliberations. As Judge Craft advised, the jury began by considering the first-degree murder charge. If everyone agreed to not guilty, they were told to move on to second degree.

According to the juror interviewed, the first vote on the first-degree charge was six guilty, six not guilty. After more conversation, there were two not-guilty votes. "One juror said he 'did not believe that a female could hold someone down and do that. He said he believed [Jennifer] would have moved.' So one juror told one juror to lay (sic) down on the floor. One juror would *show* one juror how that could happen. So we took a pencil and showed him how it could happen."

Jury instructions state that "The Jury in no case should have any sympathy or prejudice or allow anything but the law and the evidence to have any influence upon them in determining their verdict;" but the instructions made no specific mention of the word *recreate*. Thus, the jury apparently was comfortable staging a mock murder attack. Using a pencil as the weapon, the female juror re-created the attack as she imagined it happening. And she was able to convince the male juror that it would have been possible for Noura to kill Jennifer. "That first [knife wound] was where she went down. The one stab was where the coroner said it was where she couldn't be mobilized too much." She demonstrated how the assailant had anchored her weight by putting one foot on the bed, giving herself a wider reach and more stability to land the mortal blow. "I don't think there would have been a footprint on the bed if [the attacker] had been a man. Because they have more weight. They had better reach."

Then, according to the juror, [Noura] sat on the bed "and just went at it." There was a spot free of blood on the bottom sheet, and she believes that's where Noura sat to inflict the other stab wounds and cuts. "I was never—there was speculation that two knives were used—I was never convinced that two knives were used. I think you could actually make those serrated marks by rubbing or something. I was never really convinced of the two knives thing. Could've been. I wasn't there."

While reviewing the photographs of Noura's hands, the juror believes it was the jury foreperson who noticed small red marks on the side of her right hand and further noted that knives have a protruding edge designed to prevent the hand from sliding onto the blade. One juror suggested the marks on Noura's hand were caused by repeatedly hitting that small edge as she stabbed her mother. (When a juror asked a homicide detective at Noura's sentencing hearing why the red marks weren't mentioned during the trial, he said that would be "creating" evidence.)

The jury had the two knives that were entered as evidence, as well as Mark Irvin's pitching wedge, and they had questioned among themselves why they were considered relevant? They were not the murder weapons. But they used the knives to stage a re-enactment to see if the red marks would appear after a mock stabbing. Using one of the two knives from the Jackson kitchen, they wrapped a towel around the blade, and a male juror held the wrapped blade while a female juror stabbed "We counted one, two, three, we kept count. She kept stabbing as hard as she could," the juror recalled. "Then when she put her hand down they matched. They matched Noura's hand. Just that little place. And you could hear everybody go 'Oh.'"

The jury was in complete agreement about Noura's guilt, including premeditation. "It was all there," the juror acknowledged. But the antideath penalty juror and the juror known as Exhibit Man held out. The juror interviewed challenged the juror concerned about the death penalty, "I told him, 'Whenever we first sat down here, you said you could do this, and you said you could do this, and you said you could do this.' And no matter what I said, his answer was 'I can be here two weeks.'"

In the end, Noura's trial was one of Shelby County's most complicated and expensive in recent years: 810 crime scene photos, 392 exhibits and over 40 witnesses. Yet the voluminous evidence failed to produce a murder weapon or link the defendant's DNA to the crime. But the lack of forensic evidence did not forestall the jury. Some were convinced of Noura's guilt when deliberations started. The juror interviewed had decided on a guilty verdict during the first full day of testimony.

"I was sure when the neighbor [Joe Cocke] testified," she said, "and when I heard the 911 call. [Cocke] said [Noura] came over and said, 'There's an intruder in my house.' And then she led the way. I've raised kids. When you've got a girl that age, and she thinks there is an intruder in the house she—girls—do not get in front of a gun. Girls don't run into a house when they think an intruder is in there, and their mother has been killed in that manner. If a girl—if a daughter—sees her mother that violently killed, she doesn't do that. She would not have run into that house. It doesn't happen that way.

"On the 911 tape the woman said 'Has your mother been shot?' Noura said 'no.' Noura would not have known that. She couldn't have positively said 'no.' There's blood everywhere. Did Noura roll her mother over? Did she see her side? Did you see all the blood on that bed? Did you see the room? Would you have told somebody 'no'?

"You would have said 'I don't know. Please come help. I don't know what's happened.' You wouldn't have said 'no.' That was a slip of her conscious. She *knew* her mother was not shot."

Unaware of what the jury was thinking, the defense worked tirelessly to discredit and raise doubts about how CSI processed the murder scene. Crime Scene Investigator David Payment's testimony for the prosecution began the afternoon of day two and continued until late afternoon on day three. Then, for the afternoon of day three and the entirety of day four, Corder grilled Payment. His extended stay in the witness chair left everyone fatigued.

"I don't want to throw him under the bus," Helldorfer said, "but he's up all night; he's tired; he's testifying all day for a couple of days. Guy's worn out. . . . And they beat him up. They took advantage of it. And that's what they're supposed to do. When I get chewed on by a defense attorney, I expect it. If I mess up they're supposed to jump on me with both feet."

For the jury—unfamiliar with prosecution and defense tactics—half that time or even less would have sufficed. Unbeknownst to Corder, the jury quickly had surmised Payment was in over his head that day at New Haven, and they found her repeated hammering away at his errors and oversights needlessly redundant.

"I think the defense did a lot wrong, *a lot*" the juror said. "They irritated the hell out of us. There was nothing for [Corder] to put on, so she had to do a lot of face time . . . and hope something will happen. I felt like she did a lot of repeating stuff, dragging stuff on, this is this, this is this. And we knew that, and we knew this, and we knew that. Because we were tired. It went on and on. The detective, Payment. Bury the man already. And he wasn't doing anything for the jury. He did not help us. At one point I was hoping a dog would come and take her off. . . . We did two days. We did two full days of the same thing."

While the defense felt comfortable not calling any witnesses, the juror believed it made the prosecution's case "that much stronger." Corder's decision not to put on any witnesses "was a big mistake." She believes it would have made a difference. "Corder," she said, "was a smart lawyer and her closing summation—'no blood here, no blood there'—was good." But "Valerie needed more. More than Noura. She was fighting with the wind."

EPILOGUE

Noura bought cigarettes on her way home from Perry's and delayed going inside to finish one. "No smoking in the house" was another of her mom's bullshit rules, and Noura was smoldering like the ashes. The night could not have gone worse! Perry had answered her calls coolly, if he answered them at all. Her texts to him mostly were ignored. Soon after leaving his house tonight she'd called him, came right out and said she wanted to get back together. Felt awful. Like she was begging him. He blew her off. Practically hung up on her. Every place they went—Carter's, Italian Fest, even Perry's own house—failed to get her any closer to him.

She knew him well enough to know he'd moved on. It wasn't the girl he brought to Carter's place. That was a lame attempt. Deep down she admitted there was someone he really was pursuing. But whom? She remembered what it was like when he pursued her. She loved it. She realized now the times she thought she was truly happy—content—were when things were right between them. She knew she had to get that back. But with her mom barring him from their house what were the chances? Perry liked her mom, and he wouldn't come around again. Not with her mom's anger and threats against him. There were so many girls easier for him to see and be with. Noura was too much trouble for him and easily could be replaced.

The sullen mood her day started with never lifted; instead, it intensified. Plus she felt heavy with her period and the awful cramps. In her mind she looked as bad as she felt—bloated and unlovable. And she couldn't shake the night's strange undercurrent. Just a prickling vibe that would not go away. It angered her to feel such uncertainty. Whether or not others saw it she didn't know, but she'd slipped back into her too familiar role as the struggling outsider. She was on shaky ground again as the approval and acceptance she coveted receded. It was always harder for her than the others. Over and over she proved herself as their friend. When they wanted to get high, she provided. If someone wanted something a little more interesting than weed—Lortab, Xanax, even cocaine—she found a way to help them out. But still it was knock, knock, knock. If she was honest with herself, she knew the harder she tried with her friends the less successful she was, though she couldn't stop herself. Wasn't she every bit as good as the others?

It was just before 1 a.m. when she went inside. She dropped the Vera Bradley duffel she'd taken with her that night in the foyer, thought about unpacking it, but banished the notion. It made no sense to bother with that now. Later was good enough.

The rest of the Saturday night loomed before her. It was too early to be trapped in this fucking house. Thankfully she hadn't heard a noise from her mom's room. The very, very last thing she felt like now was seeing her mom, listening to her same complaints and charges. She absolutely knew she suddenly couldn't become the girl who went home at midnight as her mom demanded. She'd never done that and wasn't about to start. She made a quick call to Clark Schifani from the cordless phone in her bedroom but immediately hung up. Her mom might hear her and wake up. And no one ever answered land line calls anyway. Maybe he'd think it was her mom checking up on her?

She'd call him in a minute and see if he wanted to hang out later. She'd sneak out as she often did once she was sure her mom was really asleep. Off and on all night she'd been texting and talking with Andrew. At least he answered her. She knew he was pissed about Perry. Called her obsessed. But he'd come around. She sent Andrew another text—"Pick me up later. I gotta get out of here." He knew the drill; they'd done it enough. He'd be pretty messed up by now and ready to party. Forgive and forget.

The house with its teeming loads of junk suffocated her. Living in a Wal-Mart would be like this. In the sunroom, Noura faced bins stacked on top of bins. The contents never of interest. Crap her mom bought as if there would be happiness inside. Pathetic. Noura told her mom that time and again—the clothes hanging in plastic garment bags that no one would ever wear; the multiple sets of Williams-Sonoma cookware. A "good buy" her mom had said.

But when Noura really needed something like a nice pair of jeans, her mom went ballistic! Going on and on about frugality and excess. How could she not see how insanely absurd that was? Noura knew there must be money from her dad. She didn't believe a word of her mom's lies about that. He would want her to have that money now. To enjoy herself. Not to be at the mercy of Jennifer's miserly side; to be lectured about the cost of her haircut and a few highlights. She was eighteen, and it was her money damn it! She'd waited long enough!

Her mom. God, who was this woman? Noura felt like she was an alien. Acting like her sisters. Noura felt again the sting and humiliation of Memorial Day weekend. Having to sit silently while her mom unloaded about her to her aunt Cindy.

Enumerating all Noura's faults and failings. There was no point in sticking up for herself. They would never have listened.

Jennifer was trying to be the perfect mom now, controlling Noura's every move. She was ruining her life! Interesting, Noura thought, that she'd be like that now. Now, when Noura should have her own money and independence. It was all backward and she wasn't going to put up with it. Here came those horrible black thoughts. That anger she couldn't suppress.

It was now a little past one. She took her cell and walked quietly down the hall away from the bedrooms. She tried Clark again from her cell. No answer. Left him a quick voice message. Then she decided to send Perry one more text. She knew she shouldn't do it. He'd think she was desperate, wouldn't care, and probably wouldn't even answer. But even as she promised herself she wouldn't, she wrote—"I want to get back together. Please"—and hit send.

The quiet of the next few moments were as loud in her ears as a shrill ringing. Nothing. The silent house swallowed her. This is the way it will be from now on. Home at midnight, the rest of her friends out having fun without her, dumped by Perry, fighting nonstop with her mom about every little thing. She felt her blood boil. This had to stop. She wasn't living like that. And just that fast she realized she didn't have to. The cloying thoughts that had been haunting her for months now screamed for action. Enough! There was only one person making her miserable, and she had to get rid of her.

Noura looked around the kitchen for a knife and decided on two. She grabbed a serrated steak knife in one hand and a smooth knife both she and her mom favored because it was reliably sharp in the other. Striding now with real purpose and determination, she made her way down the dark hall with a knife tightly gripped in each hand. Her mom was strong, and

Noura knew her only chance was to surprise her as she slept. She'd probably been drinking at the wedding. Noura realized that would help. She stealthily entered the bedroom. As expected, she found her mom asleep on the left side of the bed. She crept into the room and around the bed. There was no turning back. This first blow had to end it. She dropped the steak knife and securely grasped the smooth knife. Standing directly over her mom who even in sleep made her anger flare, Noura stabbed her mom's chest with real force. The knife went farther in and easier than she could have imagined. Blood everywhere. Her mom's eyes flew open with terror, and when she recognized her daughter—God help me, Noura thought—the look of shock, astonishment, and sheer disbelief—Jennifer couldn't for a second grasp what happened to her. She raised her right hand to stop the knife from finding her again. She reached for the knife, grabbing the blade which cut her hands, and Noura drove the knife into her arm. Again, it surprised her, how deeply and easily it went through her mom's arm.

Those eyes never left Noura's face for a moment. They were fighting now. They were no longer mother and daughter but two blood-soaked enemies. Noura stabbed her face. Her cheek and her forehead. The wound to the forehead like the one to her chest and arm went deep. Noura was sure then the eyes would close. That the awful wide-eyed stare of pain and betrayal gripping her would disappear forever.

Without a weapon Jennifer had only her strength to keep her fighting. She wanted to survive this. To live. The sounds her mother made assaulted Noura, though she knew she herself was making noises too. Unrecognizable noises. Noura formed unspoken words as she realized everything had shifted. She was in charge, and she was the one doing the scolding. Stop your staring and panting! I've heard and seen enough of you. Noura answered Jennifer's piercing shrieks of pain and her heavy, labored breathing with more knife falls. The room was awash in terror.

She stabbed again and again at her mom's chest. What were minutes now? Seconds? No such thing as time. What mattered was stopping her mom. The more Jennifer moved the more Noura felt the need to land a blow. When she tried to roll on her stomach Noura stabbed her back. Then with the knife thrust downward toward her mom's feet, Noura stabbed her stomach. Damn you, stop moving! Her mom's force surprised her, and now she was trying to get off of the bed! Fuck! Noura dropped the slippery knife and with her fist tightly closed hit the side of her mom's head as hard as she could. Jennifer fell off the bed then. Catching her breath Noura thought for an instant it was over. Wrong. Jennifer was pulling herself along the floor. She wanted to reach the door, to be out of that room.

Angrier than ever now Noura reached for the steak knife. This knife at first felt secure but soon the blood made it slick too. Noura pushed her mom's head back and went for her neck and throat. A few strokes lanced Jennifer's chin. The slightest movement from Jennifer caused another round of slashes. Then the knife pierced Noura's own hand. The one holding her mom's neck back. Noura was bleeding too. She pulled her shirt off and wrapped it around her hand. Jennifer had quieted. Her grasping breaths were no longer heard. Finally, she was still.

Noura's chest was pounding. She was panting, sweating. At once those seconds and moments she couldn't find earlier were in her head. Time appeared, and Noura knew it was important to listen to it. She looked down again at her mom. Crumpled against the footboard. For a second Noura wished she could put a nightgown on her but felt that would be a mistake. Instead, she dumped the contents of a wicker basket that was near her mom's body, turned it upside down and covered her mom's head. She couldn't think with those eyes locked on her. Not once during the struggle had her mom looked away. And now even in death they found Noura. Accused her, admonished her, shamed her.

Think, think, think. Concentrate. Noura knew that every single thing she did now mattered. She found some cleaning gloves in the bathroom and put them on. It would be good if this looked like a robbery. It easily could happen in Memphis. Everyone knew that. She emptied her mom's handbag on the floor, grabbed her wallet, keys, and cell phone. The haze of the Lortabs lifted, and the violence in the back bedroom roared into reality. She made her way down the hall, took off her clothes, soaked with blood and sweat, and wrapped the two knives in the middle of the bundle. She crammed the bundle in her stuffed duffel. The new gold sandals skittered out, and she kicked them under the foyer table. She started to jam her mom's keys, cell phone, and wallet in the duffel too but hesitated with the wallet. It would have cash inside she might need. That she set aside.

Once in the shower she was relieved to see the blood grow fainter as it mixed with the water. A pinkish hue. She washed her body with care and her hair. Never could she have imagined the slick, sickening feeling of the blood. Once out of the shower she noticed the back of her left hand was still bleeding. The cut hurt, and it was deeper than she first thought. She stuck some toilet paper on it and put the cleaning gloves back on. She wrapped a towel around her body and stood trance-like for a moment until the noise of her cell phone jolted her. Noura had her sound preferences set high for texts, and the first alert sound was followed by another. The phone said 2:11 a.m.

"Out front." Still wrapped in a towel, she grabbed the duffel and flew out the front door. The duffel landed in the back of his truck.

"What the fuck?!" he demanded.

Noura stood close to the driver's side door, crazy-eyed with wet hair wearing only a towel and some kind of bizarre gloves.

"What the fuck?" he repeated.

"Get rid of that bag. Now!" She hissed. It was a command from a terrified and terrifying being. His nice buzz from earlier vanished. He noticed that in the heat and humidity she was cold, shaking. An awful sobriety descended.

"What's happened? What have you done?"

"You don't want to know. I'm telling you to get rid of that bag as fast and far away from here as you can or we are both screwed."

He looked at her again and felt the worst. Whatever she'd done had been terrible, and she'd pulled him in with her. Why was he so damn stupid? The stupid, crazy bitch! Why, why, did he always do her bidding? She backed away from the truck, and he took off. Two thoughts dominated. Get rid of the bag and get home. He warned himself not to speed, to be calm, yet his heart hammered in his chest. Mouth dry. Shaking. If I'm stopped with this bag, God knows what is coming, he thought. He focused and thought of dumpsters he would pass on his way home. One would catch the bag.

Back in the house Noura felt relief. The bag was gone. She dried her hair a little and put on clean clothes. A light-washed, short denim skirt, long-sleeved white tee shirt and grey New Balance tennis shoes. Again she forced herself to concentrate. She needed to see someone. To have someone say he or she was with her. Eric Whitaker had tried to call her earlier that night. She knew he was grounded so he'd be home. She called him to see if he wanted to hang out now. Good with him, he said. Eric's house was in Germantown and it would take her a while to get there.

Her eyes fell on her mom's wallet. She grabbed the two twenties out of it and stashed the wallet in one of the plastic bins in the sunroom. Going into the sunroom reminded her that this needed to look like a break-in. In the kitchen she found a mixing bowl and hit it hard against the middle, glass pane of the door, next to the hinge lock. She cringed at the racket it made and the noise of the shattered glass as it hit the floor. For the first time since she got home that night she remembered the little kitty. She hoped it wouldn't get cut walking on the glass.

The thought of walking out that door with her mom's body alone in there scared her. How well had she covered herself? What had she missed? She'd watched crime shows like everyone else. Weren't they super smart these days with all kinds of ways to gather evidence? Her hasty clean up probably wasn't the best, but it was done now. She pulled a gray hoodie on over the tee shirt and stuck her cell phone in her purse. A chill ran through her as it often did. Noura was always cold. Anyone who knew her knew that. The long sleeves would cover the small cut on her hand. That was the important thing. Stepping out on the front porch she turned and locked the front door.

Once in her Jeep she mentally ran over her route to Eric's. Her hand throbbed, and she knew she needed to tend to it. She would pass a Walgreens and buy first-aid supplies with her mom's cash—there would be no credit card record—take care of the wound and keep driving east. She took the gloves off before heading into the store. Fuck! It was bleeding pretty good, and she asked the cashier for some paper towels. What an odd look he gave her. It's 4:14 a.m., and this girl is asking me for paper towels? Who cares, she thought. Some stoner. God knows what he sees working in a Walgreens all night. She drove around a little before finding a convenient dumpster for the gloves.

She needed gas and time to take care of her hand. Just a little beyond the Walgreens was an All-In-One convenience store. She pulled up to the pump, used her credit card this time, and got six gallons of gas. Mostly she used the time to take care of the cut. Finally she'd staunched the bleeding. She tossed the Walgreens bag in the back of her Jeep with a lot of other junk. A second sense of relief washed over her. She could do this. It would work. She'd keep the cut discreetly out of sight with long sleeves. She'd stop by Eric's and after a bit head home. Then what she needed was someone to meet her at her house. Walk in with her. And that perfect someone was Andrew.

When Noura pulled into Eric's driveway, it was about 4:30 in the morning. He also was in his vehicle getting ready to take a friend home. Neither Noura nor Eric got out, and they exchanged hellos and goodbyes through car windows. A few seconds of talking. Noura told him she was going to meet some friends.

The composure and calm nonchalance she displayed in Walgreens and in Eric's driveway abandoned her when she thought of what awaited her at home. Noura started calling Andrew. Damn you, pick up! She was breathless, frantic, but calmed way down when she spoke to Andrew. Couldn't risk spooking him anymore than she already had. She told him she was leaving Eric's, and she wanted him to meet her at her house and walk in with her. Or to just come over and walk in if she wasn't there yet. She knew he wasn't going to do it. He ended the short conversation quickly, and she kept trying to reach him, calling his cell again and again. Finally she left a voice message, "I need to talk to you." Then she sent a text. "Answer," it demanded. Nothing.

Waves of fatigue washed over her. There was no choice but to go home. She'd go across the street to the Cockes—they were always nice—and tell them there was an intruder in the house. They'd help her. It was just shy of five in the morning when she pulled in her driveway. Noura retraced her steps to her mom's bedroom. It was real; it had happened. And at the same time as she accepted the truth of that, she found herself taking the wicker basket off her mom's head, asking her mom to talk to her.

AFTERWORD

On March 27, 2009, Judge Christopher Craft sentenced Noura Jackson to twenty years and nine months for the second-degree murder of her mother. Judge Craft looked directly at her and said, "Noura killed the only person who really loved her."

At the end of her sentence, Noura would be very close to her mother's age when she was killed. Noura is serving time at the Mark H. Luttrell Correctional Center in East Shelby County, one of two female facilities—and the less restrictive—in the state prison system. The Luttrell Center has a minimum security annex with the rest of the facility designated as close security.

Shortly after sentencing, Noura was transferred to the Tennessee Prison for Women in Nashville, Tennessee. The women's prison is the primary facility for female felons in the state and is designated maximum security. Noura spent about three months in Nashville before being moved to the Luttrell Center in Memphis. An inmate would welcome the transfer from a maximum to a close security facility, and for Noura, her Memphis support group is nearby.

Four months after the March sentencing hearing, on July 17, 2009, Judge Craft heard the defense motion for a new trial. Unmoved by their arguments, he said in summary, "Noura wove such a web of guilt from which she could not escape."

After a further appeal, The Tennessee Court of Criminal Appeals filed an eighty-two-page opinion on December 10, 2012, in which a three-judge panel affirmed the judgment of the trial court. Two of the three judges wrote a second, three-page opinion asserting that they agreed with the lead opinion except for a remark—"Just tell where you were. That's all we're asking, Noura"—made in closing arguments by state prosecutor Amy Weirich (now the Shelby County District Attorney General). The dissenting judges concluded that the remark constituted an improper comment on the defendant's choice not to testify at trial. They did not, however, believe the statement affected the verdict of the jury, and therefore did not entitle Noura to a new trial. Attorney Valerie Corder said the defense "respectfully disagrees" with the opinion and asked the Tennessee Supreme Court to accept the case for review.

On April 11, 2013, the Tennessee Supreme Court said it would hear Noura's appeal. They gave no explanation for its rather rare order, tersely presented in two sentences. Only a very small number of the appeals before the high court are granted this opportunity. At the time of the Supreme Court's announcement, it had agreed to hear nine out of 237 requests for review. The case is expected to be argued in November 2013.

APPENDIX

- **Alexandra "Alex" Kline:** Noura's friend and former classmate with whom Noura spent the day before her mother's death, swimming at another friend's house.
- **Allen E. Glenn:** Tennessee Court of Appeals Judge and author of majority opinion which upheld Noura's second-degree murder conviction.
- **Amy Weirich:** Lead prosecutor; skilled, determined, and moving up in the criminal law world; later appointed the first female Shelby County District Attorney. Two appeals court judges found that Weirich's closing arguments included "an improper comment on [Noura's] choice not to testify at trial."
- **Andrew Hammack:** An outsider among Noura's East Memphis group who described his relationship with Noura as—"friends with benefits." Conflicting accounts of his whereabouts and communications with Noura the night of the murder raised many questions and few answers.
- **Anna Menkel:** Noura's best friend whose death in an auto accident in January 2005 deeply affected her.

- **Ansley Larsson:** Mother figure to Noura who dated her son.
- **Art Quinn:** Defense counsel who told jurors in his opening statement that the trial would introduce them to a lot of "East Memphis brats."
- **Brooke Thompson:** A friend of Noura's since junior high whose party-inspired, cell phone photo on the eve of Jennifer's death became a key piece of evidence.
- **Caroline Giovannetti :** A friend of Noura's whose house Noura and others visited on Sunday afternoon, June 5, 2005, and whom Noura later sought to use as a witness to Noura's behavior the night before.
- **Carter Kobeck:** A friend in the group and possible prosecution witness, he surprised the court in jailhouse clothing after an unrelated arrest. He then assumed the role of group insider, sparking intense and curious online comments in the daily newspaper's trial blog.
- **Chris Craft:** Presiding Criminal Court Judge Christopher Craft observed Noura's peers as "very privileged, completely selfish, and out of control."
- **Cindy Eidsen:** Noura's aunt to whom Jennifer turned as a last resort to counsel Noura.
- **Clark Chapman:** Defense team's private investigator.
- **Clark Schifani:** A member of Noura's close group of friends whose involvement on the margins of the case turned out to be significant. A cell phone photo he took of Noura and three friends on Saturday evening became a key to the prosecution's case as did a phone call early Sunday to Schifani from a land line at the murder scene.

- **Connie Justice:** Memphis police detective who escorted Noura to questioning and took her witness statement on June 5.
- **Dana Fredrick, Ph.D.:** An educator, mother to two of Noura's closest friends, Lindsey and Natalie, and a confidant at whose home Noura spent considerable time.
- **David Payment:** Memphis Police crime scene officer who testified for two and a half days, explaining what evidence was collected; and during the cross-examination by Valerie Corder, answering why other pieces of evidence weren't collected and defending the integrity of the process.
- **Eric Sherwood:** Jennifer's half brother with whom she and Noura were very close. Eric had at times lived with Jennifer and Noura.
- **Eric Whitaker:** A member of Noura's circle of friends who was grounded Saturday night, June 4. The prosecution believed Noura's trip to his Germantown home around 4:30 a.m. June 5 was her attempt to establish an alibi.
- **Genevieve Dix:** An attorney and self-described best friend of Jennifer, she had known Noura since Noura was in kindergarten. Her testimony painted an unflattering picture of Noura, and her role the morning of the murder as possible legal counsel was an issue among the defense, the prosecution, and appeals court.
- **Gloria Hodge:** A longtime friend of Noura's father, Nazmi Hassanieh, who believed Noura's downward spiral began after her father's mysterious homicide.
- **Grace France:** Jennifer's sister and Noura's aunt who said her niece was "... a distant teenager and didn't want to be part of family events."

- **Jimmy Harris, Jr.:** An Arkansas farmer Jennifer married on December 23, 1992, and later divorced. Described as a gambler and a philanderer, records indicate Harris assaulted Jennifer in front of Noura meaning Jennifer had two abusive marriages both witnessed by young Noura.
- **James "Jimmy" Tual:** A longtime acquaintance of Jennifer who accompanied her on social occasions such as to a wedding the night before she was killed. He last saw Jennifer about 11:30 p.m. on June 4, 2005. Tual died April 21, 2012.
- **Joe Cocke; Rachael Cocke:** Husband, wife, and key figures in the investigation and trial who lived across the street from Jennifer. Noura's screams summoned them to the murder scene in the predawn hours of June 5, 2005, after she discovered her mother's body.
- **Joey McGoff:** Among Noura's circle of friends and buddy of Perry Brasfield. He was a member of the after party at Sophie Cooley's June 5.
- **Dr. Karen Chancellor:** The chief medical examiner for Shelby County who said Jennifer was stabbed about fifty times and that loose strands of hair were found in each of Jennifer's hands. The hairs that possibly could have been from the assailant were never tested by DNA experts.
- **Kathy Menkel:** Mother of Noura's friend, Anna Menkel, who died in an auto accident. Kathy was among the mother figures in Noura's life.
- **Kirby McDonald:** One of Noura's on-again-off-again friends and sometimes rival for Perry Brasfield. Though Kirby and Noura had perhaps more disagreements with each other than most of the group, Kirby wrote her

a note after her arrest which said "Regardless of the situation [she] loved [her] as a friend and was thinking of [her]."

- **Linda Finlay:** A fellow bond trader, friend, and confidant of Jennifer who said Jennifer's and Noura's relationship was "stormy. Jennifer tried everything to get Noura away from bad influences."
- **Marc Irvin:** Jennifer's Methodist minister boyfriend—"They fight all the time," Noura said—who called Jennifer shortly before midnight from his cell phone and abruptly hung up without leaving a message.
- **Mark Miller:** Memphis Police Lieutenant Mark Miller was the initial case coordinator, but shortly thereafter he was promoted and transferred. He coincidentally had lived years earlier at 5001 New Haven, Jennifer and Noura's home.
- **Mary Jane Fuller; Molly Fuller:** Mother and bride whose wedding Jennifer and Jimmy Tual attended on Saturday night. Mary Jane Fuller hosted the wedding reception at her East Memphis home just blocks from Noura's friend Sophie Cooley's home.
- **Max Quinlan:** Son of Ansley Larsson, a friend and boyfriend of Noura in junior high school.
- **McKenzie "Kaole (pronounced Cole)" Madison**: A consistent friend of Noura's since their freshman year of high school. Kaole encouraged Noura to stay in the Gateway home-school program.
- **Michelle Hulbert:** A Memphis Fire Department paramedic and first medical responder to enter Jennifer's bedroom. "It was odd there was a basket over the body. It seemed weird to me," she said.

- **Nazmi Hassanieh:** Jennifer's first husband and Noura's father was of Lebanese descent and had a questionable past. He was mysteriously shot and killed at his Memphis convenience store in January 2004. The case was never solved, and the death began an eighteen-month span that also included the deaths of Noura's friend, Anna Menkel, and her mother.
- **Patti Masterson:** A real estate agent, longtime friend of Jennifer's, and fellow single mother who expressed concern to Jennifer about Noura's seeming bad influence on her daughters. "As the girls grew up . . . well, it was a hard conversation to have with Jennifer," she said.
- **Perry Brasfield:** "He's like my boyfriend, but we've been on and off lately ...," said Noura, who partied with others at Perry's until after midnight the Sunday her mother was killed.
- **Randolph Reeves:** Listed as Noura's uncle and next of kin/emergency contact on her witness statement to police.
- **Rebecca Robertson:** An assistant property manager who allowed Noura to live with her and her daughter, then rented Noura an apartment for a period between the death of her mother and her arrest for murder. One day when police arrived at the apartments on an unrelated incident, Noura asked her, "Are they here for me?" A startled Robertson responded, "No, why would they be here for you?"
- **Regina Hunt:** Among Noura's potential mother figures, her place was complex. Hunt's own characterization of her relationship with Noura vacillated from scolding adult to solicitous friend.

- **Renae McMillan:** Formerly married to Noura's uncle and Jennifer's half brother, Eric, she was among the steadfast supporters of Noura during her trial.
- **Richard Raines:** On the night of Jennifer's death, he drove Noura from a party at Perry Brasfield's to her car at a previous party site at the home of Carter Kobeck.
- **Sheila Cocke:** Mother of neighbor Joe Cocke who attempted to comfort Noura after police and first responders arrived at the crime scene. Sheila lived with Joe and wife Rachael across the street from Jennifer and Noura. Sheila said she witnessed the two arguing loudly about money outside their home months before Jennifer was slain.
- **Sophie Cooley:** After Noura and the others left his house, Perry Brasfield and two friends partied with Sophie Cooley at her home until dawn on Sunday, June 5.
- **Steve Jones:** Co-counsel for the prosecution whose even, persuasive tone counterbalanced the State's more combative strategy.
- **The Reverend and Mrs. C.E. Reeves, Jr.:** Surrogate parents for a time for Jennifer and her two sisters after their parents divorced.
- **Tim Helldorfer:** A veteran Memphis homicide detective, he said, "This was out East. Good-looking, white woman murdered in a nice neighborhood. We knew it was going to be high profile. We just didn't know how high it was going to go." Helldorfer silenced the courtroom with his hand-held videotape of the crime scene walk-through.
- **Valerie Corder:** Lead defense counsel chosen by Noura over other, higher profile criminal attorneys. "She picked

Valerie because she's a mother." Noura felt Valerie would be more "hands on," said Ansley Larsson.

- **W.D. Merritt:** Memphis homicide detective who located videotape of Noura purchasing first-aid supplies at a drug store in the predawn hours the day her mother was killed. "That's when Noura's story started falling to the wayside," a juror said.
- **William "Bill" Shelton:** Another solid supporter of Noura who dated Jennifer when Noura was a toddler. He never missed one of Noura's court dates even though she hadn't been a part of his life for years.

ACKNOWLEDGMENTS

The most difficult job next to writing a book is living with the writer (some might reverse that order). For that I would like to thank my husband, Jess Bunn, who believed in this project from the outset. His support, advice, and assistance—reading, editing, and contributing the appendix—was invaluable.

I am fortunate to have friends who are attentive and gifted readers. I am indebted for their thoughtful response to my manuscript and the value they added. To my fearless first manuscript reader, Karen Wright, who tread where few would dare; to Susannah Northart for her keen insight and generous contributions with this book *and* my previous book; and James Roper, whose edit of the final proofs was the crème de la crème. It is nearly impossible to express my gratitude.

I also would like to thank Lawrence Buser, former *Commercial Appeal* reporter, for his assistance before and during Noura's trial; for helping me navigate 201 Poplar; and for introducing me to Judge Craft. As one writer borrows from another, I especially thank Larry for my book's title. In his story after Noura's February 20, 2009, conviction,

Larry wrote "Evidence showed that Noura Jackson was a distant teenager, a drug user, an underage drinker, an angry daughter and often a stranger to the truth."

Judge Christopher Craft dispelled my assumption that a criminal court judge would be unapproachable. His commitment to an open courtroom was a reflection of his confidence in the law. I personally would like to thank him for being so welcoming and helpful to me.

Photographers Lance Murphy for the evidence photographs included in the book, and Peter Scott Barta, Barta Photography, for the author photograph. For her time and talent with the cover image, Sandy Girard, creative director for Hanley Wood Marketing.

Thank you very much to those who shared their time with me in interviews: Dana Fredrick, Ph.D., Ansley Larsson, Detective Tim Helldorfer, Gloria Hodge, Andrew Hammack, Judge Craft, Linda Finlay, an unnamed juror; and sadly, Jimmy Tual who passed April 21, 2012. And individuals who helped me in other ways, Elena DiFiore, *48 Hours*, and John Russell Sadowski.

When a project is as prolonged as this one has been, expressions of interest and words of encouragement are very appreciated. Thank you to my daughter, Jordan, and son, Jeffrey, who read parts of this story in its earliest inception; and to my son, James, who is a guiding spirit.

To all of my family, especially my mother, Patricia Arch Jacobs, and father, Jerome C. Jacobs, and friends—a heartfelt thank you. With special appreciation to Sandra Baldwin for her ballet classes which always inspire. Brava!

And in memory of my uncle, Myril John Arch (1931-2013), and Charles Chunn "Chuck" Wilkinson (1953-2013). Saying goodbye is hard.

CPSIA information can be obtained at www.ICGtesting.com
Printed in the USA
LVOW06s2219160114

369813LV00002B/241/P